What others are saying about

Finding Your Life's Calling

"Everyone should read this book, because work and spirituality are essential issues in everyone's lives. The book is easily understandable to the general reader, yet it is sophisticated enough to be appreciated by psychologists and vocational counselors. Its memorable stories convey insights that are both beautiful and wise.

Charles Mintz, Actor and Writer

"*Finding Your Life's Calling* is good medicine for the soul. Greg manages to be erudite, poetic, and practical all at the same time. A very potent book."

Linda Cogozzo, Publisher, Rodmell Press

"What makes this book unique is the way it shows how work and spiritual growth are interconnected and can be integrated. It deftly weaves together historical scholarship, psychological insight, and illuminating anecdotes. This is original and important thinking."

Donald Rothberg, Ph.D., Editor, Revision Journal

"Greg Bogart's thoughts on careering are very stimulating to professional career advisors like myself. He has encapsulated concepts that I have found verified in my own experience of counseling hundreds of job seekers and career changers."

Samuel Sackett, Ph.D.
Vice-President, Bernard Haldane Associates

"Greg's findings contribute greatly to our understanding of the role of work as a central part of the spiritual path."

David Lukoff, Ph.D., Clinical Psychologist

Also by Greg Bogart

Astrology and Spiritual Awakening

Finding Your Life's Calling

Spiritual Dimensions of Vocational Choice

Greg Bogart, Ph.D.

Dawn Mountain Press
Berkeley, California
1995

Finding Your Life's Calling
by Greg Bogart

Published by
Dawn Mountain Press
P. O. Box 9563
Berkeley, CA 94709-0563
U.S.A.

Portions of this book previously appeared in the *Journal of Humanistic Psychology*.

Cover Design: Andrea DuFlon
Cover Photo: Andrea DuFlon
Editor: Nancy Grimley Carleton

10 9 8 7 6 5 4 3 2 1

First Edition
Printed by McNaughton & Gunn
Saline, Michigan, U.S.A.
Printed on acid-free, recycled paper

Library of Congress Catalog Card Number 94-093938
Bogart, Gregory C.
Finding Your Life's Calling: Spiritual Dimensions of Vocational Choice, by Greg Bogart — 1st edition
1. Psychology   2. Career   3. Spiritual Growth

ISBN # 0-9639068-4-4 (pbk.)

Table of Contents

Acknowledgments

I would like to express my heartfelt thanks to a number of people who assisted me in completing this book: Stanley Krippner, Donald Rothberg, David Lukoff, and Thomas Greening of Saybrook Institute, who made invaluable comments on earlier drafts; Linda Cogozzo, who was a constant source of advice and encouragement; and Andrea DuFlon, who contributed her artistic talents to the design of the cover. I am also quite fortunate to have worked on this project with an exceptionally patient and skillful editor, Nancy Grimley Carleton.

Many thanks to my parents, Leo and Agnes Bogart, and my sister, Michele Bogart. Chris Abajian, Rick Amaro, Bob Bartner, Mikl Brawner, Marka Carson, Nur Gale, Paul Hoffman, Michel Meiffren, Charles Mintz, Shelley Jordan Montie, Richard Rosen, Laura Shekerjian, Tem Tarriktar, and Peggy Wright have all been unfailing personal allies. I also offer grateful thanks to Stuart Gold, Frank Leana, Don Michael, Vern Haddick, Sam Heaton, Tom Miller, Robyn Sean Peterson, Nicki Sacks, Meji Singh, Jim Tucker, and Bryan Wittine for the personal and professional support they have offered.

I would like to especially thank my friend and teacher, Gayle Peterson. It is hard to adequately describe the impact that she has had on my life, but I can truly say that I would not be the person that I am without her guidance and insights.

Finally, my partner, Diana Syverud, has been both anchor and beacon to me while writing this book. Many times she has set me on the right course in my thinking and writing, and helped me regain my vision and my sense of humor. My deepest thanks to her.

True personality always has vocation, which acts like the Law of God from which there is no escape. Who has vocation hears the voice of the inner man; he is called. . . . The greatness and the liberating effect of all genuine personality consists in this, it subjects itself of free choice to its vocation.

C. G. Jung[1]

Preface

What is my calling in life? Whether we ask this question during adolescence, in college, after graduation, during midlife, or in our later years, it a central issue in the life development of most thoughtful, reflective persons. This book is written to address some of the central issues that are faced by those who actively seek a calling, work in life that integrates their spirituality with activity in the world. This topic is of particular importance in our current era, when many companies are downsizing, whole industries are relocating their operations to other countries, and many workers are being displaced from their jobs. More and more people are out of work in the traditional sense, no longer working at full-time jobs for employers but following in increasing numbers the path of self-employment and independent entrepreneurship. Many today are pursuing new, unusual, alternative professions, drawn toward careers as acupuncturists and massage therapists, as free-lance writers and photographers, as independent contractors and consultants, or as founders of publications and spiritual communities. I hope that what I have to say will be particularly pertinent to those pursuing these new vocational pathways.

This book will not repeat what so many other books have already done. There are innumerable resources available on job hunting, resume writing, interviewing strategies, and dealing with workplace politics. This book is not a substitute for going to a professional vocational counselor, taking tests to assess your vocational aptitude, and investigating specific careers by reading and taking classes. Rather this book reflects upon the inner, psychological processes involved in pursuing your true calling as a path of spiritual growth. I emphasize ways you can turn within to find your own answers. I explore the means of initiation into a calling or a central life task and the steps you need to take to make that work real in the world. I also describe some of the difficulties you might face along the way.

The book is divided into two sections. In Part I, after sharing some personal experiences, I discuss the meaning of *vocation* and trace the historical development of this concept in Eastern and Western religions. I then examine Jungian perspectives on the calling, the views of Ira Progoff and Roberto Assagioli, and Dane Rudhyar's concept of "transpersonal activity." I describe a variety of ways that a vocation may be discerned, its centrality in both traditional and contemporary religious experience, the relationship between vocation and inflation or grandiosity, and the ethical dimension of vocation. I also discuss the complexity of contemporary psychotherapy as a process that is often expected to encompass three levels of initiation that traditionally have been separated: cultural, individual, and transpersonal.

Part II presents some practical guidelines to help you find your own life's calling. I discuss eight steps of discovering and fulfilling a calling: preparation, illumination, confirmation, development, finding a shared calling (interpersonal dimensions), resolving problems and pitfalls, building a sacred vessel (spiritual and transpersonal dimensions), and defining the meaning of a personal vocation. I also tell many true-life stories that vividly portray the complex challenges of finding and achieving one's work in life. The names of the people whose stories are discussed have been changed to protect their anonymity, with the exception of a few personal friends whose full names are noted. I hope their stories, and the insights they reveal, inspire you to walk on your own path with greater clarity and joy.

Periodically I will also recount some stories about my own quest for a calling. It is somewhat ironic for me to be writing a book on this subject because it took me so long—longer than many people—to find my vocation. If my story has anything to teach it is that it can take time to find the right path and that illuminations of purpose often emerge out of some of the most confusing periods in our lives—especially if we pass through these periods with faith, courage, and a willingness to listen to the dictates of our innermost being.

Portions of my story also demonstrate the value of pursuing your calling even if it does not immediately make you rich or lead to a prestigious career. Money and power are not the only true values worth pursuing. Satisfying, interesting work that makes a positive contribution to the world can be rewarding even if it doesn't result in fame and wealth. Many people find that what is most important to them is to find a true calling, a labor of love. It is possible to earn a livelihood in some way partially or wholly unrelated to our vocation while quietly pursuing our true interests and passions. A man I know works as a psychologist by day and at night dons the cloak of a brilliant flamenco guitarist. Similarly, shamans often have other jobs that they perform when they are not engaged in healing work. I also know a number of people whose calling is to be loving, caring parents and who work in other capacities to sustain themselves so they can carry out this essential project in life. Nevertheless, for others it is essential to professionalize their life's central work and to make it their primary source of livelihood. I discuss the challenges of this process in Part II.

No matter what path you choose, it's going to take sustained effort, an ability to work within structures and routines, and a willingness to listen to your own intuition. You've got to find something you love to do and stick with it, even though it may take a long time to complete the project or work of your dreams. Join with me now to learn how you can find your true calling and the steps you need to take to make it real in the world.

Wildcat Canyon
Winter Solstice '94

PART I

The History and

Psychology of Vocation

1

Personal Background

I consciously began my spiritual journey when I was fifteen. Experiences of expanded states of consciousness and readings in psychology and mysticism inspired me to pursue the path to enlightenment. After several years of practicing meditation and yoga on my own, I found a meditation teacher and received initiation into an ancient yogic lineage. For a time I considered a monastic path, by which one signals one's total dedication to the spiritual life through renunciation of wealth, pleasures, and all egoic life projects.

During much of my teens and early twenties, I felt like "the man who fell to earth," the visitor of ancient Gnostic myths who descended from the realm of Light, forgot his true spiritual home, and became trapped in the dark world of physical matter and form.[2] As my meditation practice intensified, my interests in music, athletics, social life, and studies dried up completely. I felt in exile here on earth, estranged, purposeless, longing only for return to my divine home in the Light. Thus, I found great solace in those religious teachings that supported my sense of estrangement and gave it historical precedent—for example, the Gnostic myths, St. John of the Cross's writings about the "Dark Night of the Soul," and the austere sayings of the great Indian mystic

Ramakrishna—all of which described the traditional *via negativa*, or way of renunciation.

As my personal evolution continued, however, I began to relive other aspects of the historical evolution of religions—for example, the way the Gnostic doctrine of release from the tomb of embodied, temporal life was superseded by the Christian myth of the divine incarnation and its transformative impact on earthly history, or the way the solitary Arhat ideal of early Buddhism was supplanted by the Bodhisattva ideal of compassion and active service. Gradually I began to consider the possibility of finding what theologian Matthew Foxcalls the *via positiva*, a form of spiritual life that affirms and celebrates incarnation, embodiment, and creation itself.[3] A central ingredient of the *via positiva* is a sense of vocation, a calling in life.

At this time I also studied the life and writings of William Butler Yeats, who in his youth longed for escape to "The Lake Isle of Innisfree," and who struggled for many years to come to grips with his calling as a man of letters and of human love, as well as with his responsibilities to his homeland, Ireland. I repeatedly pondered these words from his poem "Vacillation":

THE SOUL. Seek out reality, leave things that seem.
THE HEART. What, be a singer born and lack a theme?

I questioned why I had been born with musical ability, an inquisitive mind, and an active body if these gifts were only to be renounced in favor of some higher, mystical form of experience, such as yogic *samadhi*, or God-realization. Was every facet of embodied human life simply a distraction from the attainment of such a state? Was there a way of experiencing a living relationship with the sacred dimension of life while also being at home in the world? Could I learn to bridge my personal growth—the development of my sense of identity, skills, interests, and occupational direction—with my transpersonal growth, or were these projects simply antithetical? I found myself increasingly perplexed by the challenges of trying to develop a personal identity while simultaneously trying to overcome what I viewed (following Eastern religious doctrine) as the emptiness or illusion of egoic identity.

At this time, I experienced many classical signs of the awakening of *kundalini*, the dormant evolutionary energy that, according to yogis, ordinarily lies coiled like a serpent at the base of the spine. The signs of this awakening included strange bodily movements during meditation and subjective experiences of energy currents moving through the *chakras* (internal energy centers). At first I understood these phenomena within the context of yogic teachings describing the ascent of the serpent power from the base of the spine, through the chakras, up to the top of the head, leading to the condition of liberation from bondage to the ordinary human condition.[4] I proceeded expecting that, if I practiced meditation diligently, I would soon progress through the stages of kundalini awakening toward the goal of enlightenment.

However, gradually I began to sense that the internal movements of the kundalini energy were not so much leading me upward toward a condition of release from the body and the world, but rather downward, toward a deeper, more fully crafted involvement into the physical world and personal history. My own experience seemed to suggest that kundalini was an intelligent force that had an *intention* or purpose for me and was leading me toward the creation of a vehicle in the world through which my spiritual energies could unfold. I felt, in short, that this mysterious force was trying to enrich my life on all levels, including my capacity to think, to love, to work, and to fulfill some purpose that I could not yet clearly discern.

During this period I was also exposed for the first time to the writings of the modern Indian philosopher-sage Sri Aurobindo. Aurobindo spoke of an "integral yoga" focused on the descent of a "supramental" power down into the personality that gradually transforms the instruments of senses, mind, body, and emotions. As described by Haridas Chaudhuri, a disciple of Aurobindo,

> Integral Yoga maintains that the highest goal of life is not simply the attainment of *mukti* or transcendental freedom. . . . It is not enough to effect complete liberation from nature; there is a much sublimer goal of human effort, and that is to live a life of divine activity after the attainment of individual liberation. . . . Integral Yoga. . . emphasizes the necessity of supplementing ascent by descent, negation by a deeper and fuller affirmation. [5]

The themes of a life of divine activity rather than simply achieving liberation from nature, in order to participate in the downward movement of what Chaudhuri calls the "dynamic divine," were immediately compelling to me. As I began to gravitate toward Aurobindo's Integral Yoga as a model of the transformational process I felt I was undergoing, I began to question, "What is my life's calling? For what purpose does this spiritual intelligence seek to use me?" For a long time I felt troubled by these preoccupations with questions of vocation, feeling they were a distraction or digression from attaining my ultimate goal. Gradually, however, it dawned on me that these issues—rooted in central and enduring questions of humanity's spiritual traditions—were an essential part of my own spiritual path.

A Contemporary Initiation

In 1985 I was living in a small town where I was marginally employed in a part-time clerical job, teaching yoga at a YMCA, and practicing yoga intensively. I had no profession other than that of a yogi and did not feel particularly drawn toward one. I had left behind much of my past; my future course was not clear. There were few visible signposts. I was waiting.

Then, within a brief period, three apparently separate but equally significant events altered my direction. First a dream: An older male therapist, wearing a tweed jacket, said to me with a skeptical and sarcastic tone, "So, what are you going to do, get your master's degree in yoga?"

Second, one day while relaxing a thought appeared in my awareness: "I will move to the San Francisco Bay Area and enroll in the Teacher Training Course at the Iyengar Yoga Institute." Immediately a sensation of ecstasy arose inside me. I sat up and felt my body pervaded by a powerful and blissful energy. This ecstasy lasted for close to an hour as I sat down at my desk and wrote a letter to the school.

Third, I received a call from an obscene phone caller. Despite my immediate impulse to hang up, a voice inside me distinctly and emphatically said, "Stay on the phone." I continued to talk with the man despite my feelings of revulsion. Afterward,

I felt nauseous for days, and deeply submerged memories of a traumatic episode from my childhood began to come into my awareness quite vividly. Although this experience was painful, it catalyzed an important process of emotional healing. Two weeks later, the same man called back to thank me for speaking to him. He said, "Everyone tells me what a sick person I am instead of treating me like a human being, the way you did. You helped me more than any of the therapists I've ever gone to. In fact, I think you should be a therapist."

These three events expressed in a condensed form the essence of major changes to come in my life, although I had not consciously planned or sought to make such changes. Now, ten years later, I both teach yoga and practice psychotherapy. But since that time I have often wondered about the inner voice that told me I needed to speak with the obscene phone caller and that sensed this would end up being a meaningful encounter. At the moment the man thanked me, I remembered my dream of the psychotherapist, recognized the transformative impact my conversation with the phone caller had on both of us, and knew I had found a calling. It was as if a part of me already knew that I could, should, and would become a psychotherapist, despite the fact that this was not a course of action I had ever consciously considered. Through a combination of a prescient dream, an inner voice experience, a synchronistic event, and the visitation of a mysterious energetic presence, I had undergone a modern form of self-initiation.

2

Vocation: The Life Calling

In moments such as those just described, one's path suddenly becomes clear, and one feels a new clarity, inner certitude, and rightness about the direction of one's personal life. Moreover, such experiences may also involve the mysterious sense that this direction is supported, guided, and intended by a higher source or agency, and represents the uncovering of some pre-existing order or blueprint for one's life.

Some call such experiences instances of revelation or discovering life's purpose. Others call them instances of receiving a message from God or from the unconscious. In the religious traditions of India these occurrences are known as the discovery of *dharma*, one's appropriate path in the world. In the Western religious tradition, this has been called the reception of a vocation, a calling. The centrality of vocation was evident in the lives of prophets, such as Moses, Daniel, Jeremiah, John the Baptist, and Mohammed, who felt themselves called by God to take up a specific mission. While this sense of calling may have been somewhat rare in ancient societies, it became gradually a more significant feature of the identity of modern individuals with the rise of the Protestant movement within Christianity, in which vocation became one of the central dimensions of religious life. In our era, finding one's calling is still a primary psychological need, although vocation is now often detached from the traditional religious settings in which it was once embedded. Many people, for example, undergo psychotherapy hoping it will lead them to a discovery of their true vocation.

The call to a particular vocation through a religious or spiritual revelation may fulfill three essential needs: the need to engage in meaningful social participation, the need to actualize individual potentials, and the need to receive the mandate and guidance of some higher intelligence or divine presence. Vocation may be viewed as a unifying story that brings together the social, individual, and the sacred or transpersonal dimensions of life. As such, vocation is an integrative principle that can be especially useful for those striving to coordinate the pursuit of spiritual awakening with embodied, historical, personal life in this world—in short, for any person seeking to integrate psychological and spiritual—or personal and transpersonal—growth. The principle of vocation may also enable us to overcome the privatization of religion and spirituality noted by some observers[6] by demonstrating that spirituality and mystical experiences can be, and often seek to be, focused, grounded, and expressed in concrete ways in the social world.

By *vocation* I refer to more than simply a profession, an occupation, or a work-related role, ways in which the term is usually understood. Rather, the concept of vocation suggests having a calling, a path or a lifework to accomplish, and is thus a central facet of the narrative that a person constructs to make sense of his or her personal history. While vocation may or may not correspond to our primary means of earning a livelihood, it always refers to a life project that is viewed as central to our identity.

Vocation is a pivotal part of an individual's personal myth, which psychologist Stanley Krippner describes as an imaginal narrative or statement that addresses basic existential human concerns, and that has behavioral consequences.[7] According to Feinstein and Krippner, while many collective myths have lost their power to guide and inform human lives, modern individuals can now define their own personal myths.[8] Personal myths address questions of identity (who am I?), direction (where am I going?), and purpose (why am I going there?), and fulfill the four traditional functions of myths— namely to explain the world, to guide individual development through the stages of a meaningful life, to provide a foundation for fulfilling social relationships, and to address the individual's spiritual longings and need for a sense of cosmic perspective.[9] Thus, we may view vocation as a particular form or aspect of personal myth that is specifically related to our sense of calling. Personal myths often clarify the individual's relation to higher powers, or the cosmos.[10] Thus, myths of vocation are particularly important, as they specifically emphasize our relation to those powers and the way in which we interpret our actions as impelled by them.

A sense of vocation is derived from an act of self-interpretation and reflects a subjective sense that our lives and actions are guided by, and are, in some sense, the unfolding of a patterned personal destiny. In addition, vocation may emerge as a result of religious, mystical, or transpersonal experiences that specifically take the form of a revelation of individual life purpose. This suggests that there may be a particular class of transpersonal phenomena that have (or can be interpreted as having) a dimension that refers to *personal* direction. In many instances it seems that mystical or transpersonal awakenings seek expression through a personal life project or seem to contain implicit directives for such a project. A calling may thus be viewed as an integrative experience bridging social action, individual development or self-actualization, and spiritual or transcendental concerns. Moreover, the theme of vocation provides one way in which we may *interpret* and *personalize* spiritual or religious experiences. In short, *vocation* is a narrative form or mythic construct describing an individual's sense of personal identity or project in life as this is revealed through experiences that can be characterized as spiritual or transpersonal.

3

Historical Development of the Concept of Vocation

The concept of vocation emerged out of a variety of historical influences. In ancient India, a principle related to vocation was found in the concept of *dharma*, which was central to religious and spiritual life. Dharma originally referred to ethical conduct, carrying out one's mandated social role, and fulfilling one's position in the caste system. According to Richard Lannoy,

> Dharma consists of three categories: the eternal or *sanatana dharma*, principle of harmony pervading the entire universe; the caste *dharma* (*varnashrama-dharma*), relativistic ethical systems varying from caste to caste; and *svadharma*, the personal moral conduct of the individual, close to our "conscience." [11]

In India your occupation was traditionally determined by social class and family custom, not by personal choice. You did a job that was appropriate to your social class, and you didn't try to rise above your caste because your social position was believed to be determined by your *karma*, your past actions. Dharma was a principle that in some respects circumscribed people's activities, but it also provided a sense of order in life because you knew who you were supposed to be. You were a shoemaker, a weaver, a dyer, or a tailor because your father was one. Because dharma also represented the cosmic order, to act in accordance with one's social role was to act in accordance with the universal order of things.

Over the course of time, the concept of *dharma* came to imply much more that just conforming to the moral standards and dictates of the social order. In the popular religious-spiritual text, the Bhagavad Gita, for example, a profound tension is evident between traditional dharma or caste duty and an individual's *svadharma*, literally "one's own dharma," the sense of personal identity and the path in life that one feels one ought to follow. The protagonist of the Gita, Arjuna, is in conflict between his caste duty as a warrior to fight a war that he feels is futile and his own desire to retreat from the battle. Krishna counsels Arjuna to fulfill his dharma by fighting without attachment to the fruits of his actions. In the words of Nicolas, "The Bhagavad Gita offers us a model of human freedom within human determinism; of freedom within socially controlled situations." [12] The essence of Nicolas 400-page treatise on the Gita is that this freedom is found through acts of self-interpretation that enable one to give meaning to one's life (individual svadharma) in relation to one's socially and historically determined circumstances (socially mandated dharma). This act of self-interpretation is what I call defining one's calling, and it is an act that may involve a profound tension between conforming to socially defined roles or activities and following one's individual calling, while also trying to live in accordance with the universal dharma, what some might call "the will of God."

In the Bhagavad Gita, the concept of dharma is associated specifically with the path of *karma yoga*, the path of sacred action, which can be viewed as the enactment of one's calling. While one may be called primarily to a life of contemplation rather than to a life of outward, active service, a sense of calling may also lead to pursuit of karma yoga, that is, work or action that is felt to be sacred, an expression of a higher will or divine intention. To be true karma yoga, action must be impelled not by personal desire but by the divine spirit working out through the individual its purposes in the world.[13] In this sense, dharma also has a transpersonal dimension in addition to its social and individual aspects. As we will see later, philosopher Dane Rudhyar has discussed karma yoga in a contemporary context as the path of "transpersonal activity." In my opinion, dharma and the path of karma yoga, or sacred action are domains of spiritual life that have largely been neglected in the contemporary new age movement and the field of transpersonal psychology relative to the attention other topics, such as altered states of consciousness, have received.

In Western religions the principle of the calling has been central. In the Judeo-Christian tradition, the concept of calling or vocation has two chief theological meanings: the call by God to eternal life and the occupation or place in society to which a person is assigned by God. In the Old Testament, various prophets heard the voice of God commanding them to speak to the people. Thus, originally the call was given only to special individuals who had the mission of being God's voice or mouthpiece. But in the Old Testament the call in a broader sense referred to the call of God that was extended to the nation of Israel, a covenant demanding obedience to God's commandments. While God sometimes called individuals to particular roles as prophets, kings, military leaders, and priests, the communal emphasis of the calling remained primary.[14]

In Christianity, the call did not mean a divine exhortation to return to a collective covenant but a call to repent and embrace the kingdom of God as individuals. The call in early Christianity was to approach the kingdom of heaven in faith, to turn toward the eternal life promised in the Gospels. This was a spiritual call, a call to turn toward the eternal presence of God.

In the Middle Ages, when the growth of monasticism within the medieval church fostered a sense of separation between spirituality and worldly labor, monks considered their calling to the contemplative life to be superior to ordinary occupational labor. Later, however, theologians John Tauler and Martin Luther declared that common works have spiritual significance and dignity. Eventually, the term *calling* came to be applied to secular occupations, which could be viewed as divinely ordained. Luther emphasized the primacy of faith over works, which implies that no works are in themselves better than others in the eyes of God. However, to Luther, vocation was "a task set by God" that must be obeyed, not a path selected by free human choice, as humanist thinkers would soon contend. Renaissance humanist philosophers like Erasmus increasingly emphasized the discovery of one's own character and talents—the deliberate choice of a way of life and a career consistent with one's nature, aptitudes, and constitution.[15]

The humanist vision of the individual as self-determining was quite antithetical to the doctrine of vocation set forth by theologian John Calvin, to whom worldly success became a visible sign of God's grace and the certainty of election to salvation. Harry Goldman writes,

> For Calvin. . . the *vocatio* is from God, mediated through men. . . . But unlike Erasmus's genus vitae, it is set *against* one's own nature and inclination; yet as a divine command it is at once irresistible and *imposed* on our nature. God works *in spite* of our natural inclinations. This shows the difference between the choice and the call, between choosing and being called. . . . Vocation is the office or station in which God places us for his employment, not for our enjoyment.[16]

These distinctions between Calvinist and humanist perspectives highlight the tensions implicit in the contemporary meaning of vocation, for we have inherited both Calvinist and humanist conceptions of vocation and often experience a calling in life as paradoxically both freely chosen but also ordained and commanded—if not by the will of God then by some mysterious inner law.

According to Max Weber's classic study,[17] the concept of calling became increasingly linked to the growth of economic and entrepreneurial activity. In Weber's view, the Calvinist doctrine of the calling—the idea that selfless service in a calling could provide justification or salvation—was central to the development of the modern personality. He contended that in the Protestant Reformation a new form of self, ascetic and self-denying, had developed built on the calling. Weber believed that this new ascetic self endowed the first great capitalist entrepreneurs with the energy to resist tradition and become innovators through rationalized labor. Labor in the calling and service to an ultimate ideal became the source of life's meaning and of a new type of person, one preoccupied with rational activity devoted to increase of capital, scrupulous avoidance of spontaneous enjoyment and pleasures, and one for whom making money is an end in itself.[18] The intense dedication to proving one's worth to God through tireless, pious, and methodical labor, self-subjugation, and accumulation of wealth led to growing preoccupation with the self, a new spirit of individualism as well as a spirit of capitalism.

Weber viewed vocation as a major source of the drive to control the world through rationalized enterprise that characterizes both modern Western civilization and modern individualism. Weber[19] contended that the Western notion of vocation differs from the Hindu principle of dharma and has enduring significance for modernity because of its capacity to shape and fortify the self to transform the world, rather than simply to adapt and accommodate itself to the orders of the world. He also felt that "the return to the individualism of life in the calling" was an appropriate response to "the collapse of a shared or 'collective' sense of meaning in life," one providing renewed sanctification of self and work.[20] According to David Ingram, the new person who was created though the ascetic ideal of vocation possessed a new awareness of the possibility of progress through rationality, and a capacity for analytic reasoning that helped define modernity.[21]

However, while the notion of vocation may have done much to shape the modern character in a positive sense, it may also lie at the root of the cultural crisis of modernity. For the growth of vocation was associated with the breakdown of traditional religious beliefs and ensuing moral relativism, the decay of the traditional ethics of responsibility and universal reciprocity, and the enthronement of individual economic advancement. Ascetic vocationalism was also characterized by ever-more specialized work requiring renunciation, leading to a deepening mechanization, bureaucratization, and dehumanization of modern life and labor. Moreover, the rational-purposive activity that characterized the ceaseless and increasingly specialized labor of modern workers creates an inner hunger that is only vitiated through an insatiable desire to enjoy the material products of capitalist production. The sacrifices demanded by vocation are thus, in Ingram's view, at the root of "the irrational confluence of asceticism and consumerism." [22]

Weber made a crucial point in arguing that the modern revival of the Reformation principle of vocation may be an important means of resanctifying identity and labor in a world devoid of persuasive shared beliefs or values. But, alternatively, it might be possible for us to revive an awareness of the principle of vocation in a manner that is not predominantly oriented toward activity motivated by a desire to control the external world, and that does not fuel compulsive consumerism—which Ingram describes as a backlash against the sacrifices demanded by ascetic pursuit of vocation.

Just as the Protestant conception of vocation represented an evolution beyond the culture-bound conception of dharma that generally prevailed in Hinduism, we need to evolve beyond the individualism implicit in the Protestant vocation. Perhaps we could pursue our personal callings without exacerbating the ecological destruction and materialistic excesses to which a sense of vocation has at times contributed. Through a curious turn of the spirals of history, the next step in our understanding of vocation may come once again from examining the doctrines of an Eastern religion, in this case, Buddhism. In my view, the more ethical and communal concepts of dharma that prevailed in Buddhism could provide a healthy counterbalance to the predominantly individualistic emphasis of the Western concept of vocation.

Dharma and Engaged Buddhism

Many contemporary Westerners, sensing the emptiness of a life focused solely on the quest for material gain, have sought guidance from Eastern spiritual traditions, especially Buddhist teachings. In Buddhism, the term dharma is central and has several meanings. On the one hand, dharma refers to each aggregate or conditioned factor of existence, "impersonal forces" constituting all apparent entities.[23] Dharma also signified the doctrine, the teachings, and the path of Buddhism, as well as the truth to which those teachings point. Thus, dharma refers to a spiritual way of life that is in alignment with the doctrines of Buddhism. The Buddhist dharma in this second sense includes teachings about impermanence, selflessness or egolessness (anatta), and the "codependent origination"—or interdependency—of all entities and events. Awareness of the dharma leads one to do those actions called forth by the universe, including compassionate, selfless action intended to serve and relieve suffering. Thus, from a Buddhist perspective, the true meaning of dharma as a calling or path in life is not found in the individualistic orientation that vocation came to assume in Western nations, but rather by coming into right relationship with the condition of truth: the interdependence and codependent origination of self and world. Dharmic action, from this perspective, is action that links self and world.

While Buddhism is often thought of as a "personal, privatized" religion of solitary monks meditating to achieve individual enlightenment, a contemporary movement called "engaged Buddhism" promotes a direct involvement with moral issues and social injustice and recognizes a need to make a "relevant, situational response" to the sufferings in the world.[24]

> Buddhist and other kinds of spiritual paths are not about social liberation but about human liberation, about release of human potential trapped in the delusive suffering which arises from the root human condition. Hence they are also about social liberation as an integral though dependent part of this process. [25]

Buddhist social activism is based on the Buddhist analysis of suffering and delusion, which are seen as rooted in the desire to acquire power, prestige, wealth, and sensual pleasure, to possess and cling to all things that strengthen a separate sense of self. Buddhist analysis of craving and its results can also be carried beyond the individual level into an examination of patriarchal social dynamics, abuses of authority, domination of the environment, and socioeconomic oppression.

Engaged Buddhism counteracts these personal and social tendencies through reverence and gratitude for all things, the avoidance of harming others, and compassion for all. In contrast to the dualistic view of a separate self existing in opposition to an objective world, Buddhism is based on the view that self and object exist in a dialectical unity, a reality that can only be perceived when one is "unweighted by strong self-need." [26] Through moral and meditative mind training, Buddhism seeks to overcome the pernicious dualism that gives rise to the domination by social elites of nature and of other social groups. According to Jones, only spiritual conviction and training of this kind have the strength to bring about the shift beyond our root fear, our acquisitiveness, and our aggressive, often xenophobic identification with our tribe, race, or nation.[27]

Buddhist morality is intended to cultivate good character, and is part of a system of spiritual training through which "an unalienated and intrinsically good personality" will ripen.[28] Dharma as a spiritual path or way of life involves practicing certain precepts that are intended not to constrain but to guide one into a condition in which one does no harm to others. These precepts include avoiding killing or violence; not taking what is not given, and being generous and nonacquisitive; abstaining from lies, malicious gossip, verbal abuse, and from what Buddhist teacher Christopher Titmuss calls "sexually exploitive activities"; pursuit of right livelihood, and avoiding vocations that are harmful to humans and nature; remaining open-minded, nondogmatic, and noncoercive of others; remaining aware of the suffering in the world and not closing one's eyes to it; living simply and sharing one's time, energy, and material resources with those who are in need; releasing anger and hatred and looking at others with "the eyes of compassion"; practicing mindfulness; striving to relieve human suffering by all possible skillful and expedient means.[29]

The traditional Buddhist doctrine of the oneness and interconnectedness of all beings has most recently influenced the movement known as deep ecology, which Jones describes as

> a mentality in which all beings are seen as having equal rights to their own forms of unfolding and realization within their biosphere, whether it be a tract of woodland, human society, or the whole planet. Deep ecology is about the cultivation of a consciousness so that, in Arne Naess's [the founder of deep ecology] words, "with maturity, human beings will experience joy when other life forms experience joy, and sorrow when other life forms experience sorrow." [30]

From this perspective, the concept of dharma also suggests protecting the right of other beings to unfold their own existence. In the contemporary setting, then, any truly dharmic way of life should be based on a fundamental "respect for the things we must consume and destroy in order to live, and a lean, aware frugality in our use of resources." [31]

Buddhist doctrines have led to development of a new awareness of land stewardship, of a sense of local place, and of innovative agricultural methods, all of which could be important foundations for a future society of more self-reliant communities. Engaged Buddhist principles have also inspired the formation of many organizations and movements, such as: Cooperatives dedicated to economic self-help and self-reliance, including grassroots social change movements in Asia, especially in Sri Lanka, Thailand, and Vietnam; the Buddhist Peace Fellowship, dedicated to promoting peace and protection of all beings, understanding the roots of violence, and working toward the ending of exploitation of all beings; social service projects and hospices like the Hanuman Foundation's Dying Project; strategies of radical activism utilizing Buddhist principles of peacemaking and nonviolence, often involving nonviolent direct action, "which recognizes the common humanity of the adversary and his dignity and autonomy"[32] ; efforts to change social policies, practices, and institutions regarding disarmament and defense policy, Third World poverty, environmental protection, women's rights, prisoners of conscience, and persecution of ethnic minorities.

The way of life elucidated by engaged Buddhism can provide us with a useful alternative to the model of a calling derived from the Protestant concept of vocation. Many of the excesses fueled by vocation as described earlier could be mitigated to a large degree by consideration of the ethical and political perspectives of engaged Buddhist teachings. The contemporary engaged Buddhist perspective suggests that in addition to the societal and individual types of vocation, there may also be what I will call a transpersonal type of vocation. Transpersonal vocation in the Buddhist sense would refer to a life project that is driven not by egoic motivations, but by the motivation to express compassion, relieve suffering, and act in ways that serve others and that respect the existence of all life forms. Therefore, it may be seen as a form of vocation that is based on self-transcending action in the world.

4

Contemporary Dimensions of Vocation

While some of its traditional meanings may have changed, vocation has remained a central facet of modern psychological life. The Hindu concept of dharma suggests that the fulfillment of one's socially defined place in the world can lead to "transcendence of individuality into universality, into *moksha*, release from personal existence, the goal of Hinduism."[33] Nevertheless, dharma, based on impersonal social principles, is not chosen but rather is a product of one's position at birth. In contrast, the Western sense of a calling implies that one is called by a personal, individual, inner voice. This more personal inner voice or calling is the source of the kind of assurance found in Protestantism that there is "a specific social task for each person to live out, as an expression of God's Will acting through him or her." [34] It was also this personal inner voice that empowered individuals like Gandhi and Thoreau to commit acts of civil disobedience dictated by their own conscience. In Paul Fleischman's view, however, both concepts, dharma and vocation, refer to

the yearning for a calling, for a task that fulfills the world as it moves forward in one's own life, for a role that interlocks with the roles of all other men and women and with the goals of the creative powers that brought life into the world.[35]

In this book, I will use both terms, dharma and vocation, in this sense of a fundamental calling, task, or role, characterized by a firm conviction about one's place in the universe, and the either socially or subjectively defined purpose and mission of one's life.

The concept of vocation, while it has generally become more modestly used as a term referring to an individual career, is in a broader sense roughly equivalent to what Ira Progoff calls "the opus of a life. . . , a single directive principle unifying one's inward and outward life." [36] Progoff has described how—through initiatory experiences or dreams—an individual may discover images of potentialities that are capable of becoming concrete. Living in accord with such images enables one to "restructure and rededicate one's life" so that "a larger than personal factor expresses itself in one's affairs." [37] The "life task," a combination of outer work and inner opus, is an image that can be translated into "a specific path of activity that will indicate the particular form and content of the life."[38] The life task is unique for each individual, he writes, "inherent in the seed of his being and the embodiment of his personal destiny." [39]

Progoff's statement that the life task is inherent needs to be qualified slightly, for theories of intrinsic individual qualities may be subject to the criticism that they espouse the tenet that human nature is presocial and separate from culture, and that humans have an inherent inner nature that must struggle to realize its capabilities by peeling away social restraints and inhibitions.[40] Such theories provide the basis for an overly "subjectivized world view. . . . in which culture and social structure play a very small role in either defining human potential or enhancing its fulfillment." [41]

Some have proposed a more balanced view, namely that vocation or dharma is both inherent *and* developmentally (i.e., socially) acquired. Psychoanalytic pioneer Heinz Kohut for example, acknowledges the existence of "innate potentialities" that contain a "blueprint for life" in the nuclear self. Yet Kohut writes that the child's "innate potentialities. . . , merging with the expectations of the self-object, are the point of origin of the infant's primal rudimentary self." [42] According to Andrew Samuels, Jungian psychologist Michael Fordham has also postulated "a primary self integrate, present at birth, which on meeting a correspondence in the environment, commences a rhythmic cycle of deintegration and reintegration." [43] Both Kohut and Fordham suggest that the potentialities that may be inherent at birth must meet "a correspondence in the environment." Thus, vocation may be, in a sense, both innate and socially constructed. That is, the self must adapt and develop its innate potentialities within the context of social-environmental conditions.

Individuation and the Guidance Self

The concept of vocation or personal calling is implicit in Carl Jung's theory of the Self, which Jung calls "a construct that serves to express an unknowable essence which we cannot grasp as such, since by definition, it transcends our powers of comprehension. It might equally be called the 'god within us.'"[44] Edward Whitmont comments,

Here. . . there is reference to an undefinable essence, which manifests itself as thematic form-setter for the empirical person, unrepresentable as such except through symbol. This particular entity of the implicate order has been called Higher Self or Spirit Self in esoteric tradition. I prefer to call it Guidance Self. This Guidance Self is something other than the psychoanalytical self, which refers to the empirical personality and its complexes. . . which in esoteric tradition has been called "lower self." The Guidance Self . . . is of the nature of archetype. It includes the notion of symbols of karma or destiny. As archetypal order it can be postulated as dialectically interacting with complex self or ego. . . . Transformation and healing are brought about by being moved and touched by, and by striving to actualize—that is, to personalize—the significance of the transpersonal or archetypal elements that arise from the Guidance Self. [45]

The intuition or discovery of a vocation, the opus of the life, emerges into consciousness through the Guidance Self in the form of archetypes, "symbols of karma or destiny," which must be lived out. The influence of the Guidance Self is not just experienced as the mystical visitation of a numinous presence or Reality but as the revelation of a patterned personal destiny, of an ordered universe and one's intended place within it.

According to Nathan Schwartz-Salant, individuation is a process in which "a far greater wholeness"—which he calls "the Numinosum"—incarnates into space-time reality. This process has also been referred to in alchemy and in Jungian psychology as the *conunctio*, a union between the archetypal image and the material life of the body.[46] Schwartz-Salant describes how one may evolve from a stage in which an Old Testament–type God image (perceived to be outside the person) is grasped in a state of archaic identity, to a stage in which there begins to be "an indwelling of this Spirit such that a psychic center, a Self, is formed." Development from the patriarchal God image toward the dimension of inwardness bestows a new sense of *chosenness*, enabling one to act feeling connected to "the vast energy sea" or "the oneness of God," and able to employ one's creative gifts for one's own purpose.[47]

Here we see beautifully expressed some of the essential insights of Jung's legacy. From this perspective, the symbol of dharma is an internal, personalized God image that dwells within us, awaiting discovery and incarnation. The discovery of this internal God image is a central dimension of human psychological life, the source of vision and inner guidance that—within the context of particular environmental and social forces—gets translated into activity, meaningful work, or spiritual practice, the central task that fulfills the opus of the life.

5

Vocation and Initiation

How does one discover one's life opus? While I will continue to discuss finding a vocation in general, here I will begin to focus more specifically on instances in which the discovery of a life calling emerges as a result of some illuminating religious, spiritual, or mystical experience. In this section, I will explore six major ways in which we can perceive our vocation: external initiation, dreams, inner voice phenomena, synchronistic events, deliberate construction of personal myths, and the use of oracular or symbolic methods. I also believe that other experiences could be added to this list—for example, shamanic journeys and traumatic life events such as near death episodes. In Part II, some of these topics will be discussed in greater detail.

Of course, some individuals arrive at a sense of vocation gradually in the course of maturation, rather than through a single, noteworthy event, while some people never do arrive at a sense of vocation, whether for personal reasons or due to social constraints. Here, however, I am concerned with instances of transformative mystical or transpersonal illuminations in which a sense of vocation suddenly becomes clear. While it is possible to find a spiritual sense of calling in less dramatic ways, I am examining vocation in the context of such experiences because I believe it is here that the deepest impact and implications of vocational discovery may be most clearly evident.

Rites of Passage

One of the primary ways of discovering one's vocation or life task is through rites of passage—ritual forms that have traditionally provided experiences through which a person can discover his or her guiding myth or true identity. Even in cultural contexts in which a guiding myth is part of the tribal or cultural background rather than something an individual "discovers," rites of passage enable initiates to discern an affinity with particular totems, spiritual clans, or social roles. There are three basic stages to these rites: separation, liminality, and reintegration.[48] The initiate is separated from the community and from his or her accustomed social role and is placed in a situation of profound fear and uncertainty, usually involving physical deprivation or trauma. If successful, the initiation climaxes in a display of sacred objects, transmission of a body of mythology or religious doctrine, or a visionary or auditory experience in which significant aspects of the initiate's identity, destiny, and vocation are revealed. Finally, the initiate emerges with a new myth, a set of guiding beliefs and assumptions that will shape his or her awareness and actions when he or she returns to the community. As James Hall puts it, "Initiation is not an end in itself but a beginning. It. . . moves the ego across a threshold into a new

form, introducing new tasks and new goals of individuation."[49] And Louise Mahdi writes,

> The arcane knowledge obtained in the liminal period is felt to
> change the inmost nature of the neophyte, impressing him, as a
> seal impresses wax, with the characteristics of his new state.
> It is not a mere acquisition of knowledge, but a change in being.[50]

Some rites of passage, for example puberty rites, focus upon
enculturation, a new sense of responsibility for carrying out
certain culturally mandated, role-appropriate behaviors,[51]
while others, such as the Native American vision quest, focus
on individuation, the discovery of personal identity.[52] A third
kind of rite of passage is found in mystery religions and
spiritual traditions in which the goal is self-transcendence or
ego death and rebirth—for example the Eleusinian mystery
rites,[53] or the rite of *sannyas diksha*, through which a spiritual
aspirant in India symbolically dies to the world in the course
of ordination into the order of renunciate monks.[54]

It is important to note the subtle difference between receiving
an initiation by elders into the mythology governing social
existence in a traditional society and having a new mythos
revealed from within in a more personalized rite like the vision
quest. Whereas the former process calls forth obedience and
adherence to a set of culturally defined myths, in the vision
quest one receives direct communication with the Spirit,
spirits, or ancestors that reveals a new vision and a new story
of what kind of person the seeker is supposed to become.

Most initiations involve some mixture of both external
instruction and inner illumination. For example, an initiate in a
mystical order may be instructed in certain techniques and
then sent off to practice them until a personal experience of

illumination is ignited. Later, the instructor may interpret the novice's visions or realizations. Similarly, a person going on a vision quest is given instructions before embarking on "the wilderness solitude" that (ideally) culminates in a psychological death and rebirth in which guidance, vision, and power are received from helping spirits.[55]

The vision quest could be considered the prototype of all initiations emphasizing inner guidance regarding individual dharma, identity, or life path. The evolution of a rite of passage that allows an individual to temporarily step beyond the bounds of culture and to confront the elements of nature, the spirits, and one's own essential nature without interruption yet with full societal sanction and protection represents one of the greatest contributions of Native American cultures to the human heritage. Such a rite is an expression of a culture's respect for the autonomy of the individual and the need to find—inscribed in internal recesses—a vision of his or her essential nature and an awareness of a greater spiritual reality. The vision quest reflects the knowledge that allowing an individual to have glimpses of transcendence, vision, or the presence of other dimensions of existence may ultimately and paradoxically renew participation in culture. For not only is the successful vision quester vouchsafed a vision of his or her unique individual name, identity, or mission, but the raw encounter with oneself and the universe in solitude bestows a new appreciation for the familiar and safe structures of society, without which one would be, in effect, a defenseless creature in the jungle.

The Need for Self-Initiation

Many have noted the breakdown in our culture of traditional rites of passage that bestow this revelation of inner guidance leading to awareness of the individual's life task. Robert Moore notes our current failures in ritual leadership, the inadequate provision for initiation in transitional states, and contends, "The psychosocial containment and leadership that are necessary components of effective initiatory processes are absent." [56] Moore argues that personal or social changes occurring outside of a context of containment are usually, if not always, superficial in nature or abortive in consequences. "Deep structural change," he writes, "requires a reliable psychosocial framework, the facilitation of a holding environment that can help individuals and groups tolerate the terrors of change." [57]

Virginia Hine contends that there is a need to internalize and personalize the function of initiation by adopting "self-created ceremonies of passage" to mark various milestones and transitions, such as leaving home for the first time, graduation, severance of a love relationship or divorce, incorporation of a stepchild or stepparent into a blended family, retirement, or preparation for death.[58] According to Edith Sullwold, "The need for such ritual actions is so profound. . . that. . . even without previous instruction or experience these ritual forms and symbols can be created from within the psychic structure of an individual." [59] Even if an external ritual is not utilized, the unconscious mind engages in its own spontaneous form of initiatory activity. As Anthony Stevens wrote,

The attainment of a new stage of life requires that the initiation symbols appropriate to that stage must be experienced. If culture fails to provide these symbols in institutional form then the Self [within] is forced to provide them *faute de mieux.* [60]

Dreams of the Self
and the Construction of Personal Myths

Dreams are one of the primary means through which the inner Guidance Self reveals "the archetype of initiation." [61] According to Jung, the presence and guidance of the Self may be discerned through those dreams featuring the symbolic form of "a God or a Godlike human being, a prince, a priest, a great man, an historical personality, a dearly loved father, an admired example, the successful older brother—in short, a figure that transcends the ego personality of the dreamer." [62] I have found that women often perceive the Self in the form of corresponding feminine figures, such as Princess, Priestess, or Great Mother. Jung has also suggested that the Self may appear through abstract images, such as mandalas, or in the form of valuable or sacred objects, such as stones, jewels, and rings.[63]

I believe that images of the Self in dreams may possess attributes indicative of the particular qualities seeking expression, embodiment, and incarnation through a particular individual. For example, consider the dream I described at the beginning of this book. This dream featured a figure who both made a statement implying a specific directive intended for me, and who also embodied some of the attributes of professional stature and a well-defined social role that I needed to acquire for my personal maturation.

The wisdom of dreams can be used to consciously construct new personal myths that contain images of vocation. Dreams are a crucial means of bringing one's personal myths into awareness and changing them. In their personal mythology process, Feinstein and Krippner[64] utilize ritual and dreams to heighten awareness of old, inadequate personal myths, to bring new alternatives into awareness, to resolve conflicts between competing mythic structures, and to deepen commitment to acting on the new myth in daily life.

The Inner Voice

Another crucial source of guidance from the Self, widely reported in many cultures and periods of history, is the experience of an inner voice, for example, the apparently prescient voice that told me to stay on the phone with the obscene phone caller. According to Myrtle Heery ,

> The term "inner voice" refers to a significant subjective experience—the actual perception of a voice speaking internally and/or a vaguer "felt sense" of some inner communication. Just as the external voice communicates between one human being and another, the inner voice may communicate intra-psychically between one level of the psyche and another.[65]

Many persons, she writes, describe the inner voice as "a strong, positive directive force in their lives," a source of conviction and authority, which gives them inner certainty or a feeling of a "pull" or "call" from a higher principle. Heery notes that the concept of a call is akin to the Hindu concept of dharma the law of nature, which if violated causes serious imbalances.

Synchronicity and the Use of Symbolic Methods

Jung also noted the importance of synchronistic events, meaningful coincidences between outer events and inner events that seem to provide direction, guidance, or insight.[66] These are events that seem to be too uncannily pertinent to one's situation to be purposeless or merely coincidental. Recall the way my conversations with the obscene phone caller, which concluded with the caller telling me I should be a therapist, came soon after the dream of an older therapist who had a similar message for me. One could say that the experience I had on the telephone was an opportunity for me to more clearly "get the message" of my dream.

In his essay on synchronicity, Jung also discusses astrology at some length.[67] The use of oracular and symbolic methods such as astrology, Tarot cards, and the I Ching, all of which have enjoyed a widespread resurgence of popularity in recent years, is another perennial method of attempting to discern dharma or the direction of the individuation process. Rather than being primitive superstitions, mere fortune-telling techniques, or forms of magical thinking, each of these methods has been used for centuries to help human beings ponder their place in the universe and the meaning of events. All of these methods are means of awakening our innate, intuitive knowledge about the direction of our lives. Astrology, in particular, is based on the belief that each individual is born with a particular purpose or set of tasks to accomplish that is symbolized by the positions of the planets at birth. According to the philosophy of Dane Rudhyar, every entity arises as a potential fulfillment or response to a need of some greater Whole.[68] So, too, each person's birth is a potential response to the needs of his or her tribe, nation, or humanity as a whole at a given time and place. Rudhyar argued that astrology should be approached not as a predictive method, but as a *symbolic language* that provides an archetypal representation of an individual's potentials and the steps needed to actualize them.[69] Reflection on the birth chart can be a powerful means of discerning a personalized image of a calling, the purpose of the individual's life.[70]

Vocation, Initiation, and Psychotherapy

We have seen that even though cultural mechanisms for affecting initiation into personal vocation are somewhat in decay, the "archetype of initiation" still seems to be operative through the means I have identified (as well, perhaps, as through other means that I have not identified). Nevertheless, it seems that most persons seek—and need—some kind of interpersonal matrix to support and guide the process of initiation.

Robert Moore views psychotherapy and pastoral counseling as among the few remaining settings in which contemporary individuals can receive the guidance of elders through the transitional space of renewal that rituals traditionally provided.[71] I agree with Moore and would like to discuss some issues that have been raised for me, personally, by my attempts as a psychotherapist to provide this kind of ritual leadership for my clients. In my opinion, contemporary psychotherapy is a particularly complex affair, due to the fact that it is often expected to provide *all three* functions of rites of passage, namely enculturation, individuation, and transcendence.

For example, a forty-year-old man named Dave feels socially useless and isolated, lacks a clear direction, and is "longing for God." He is highly intelligent, has traveled widely, and has seen many gurus. His quest for enlightenment, however, has not eradicated his feeling of not fitting in, of having no place or meaningful function in the social world. He is rootless and feels an underlying emptiness. He reports that what scares him most is to think that he might not have a destiny, a calling. He comes to therapy seeking initiation, a rite of passage that will enable him to discover his vocation, his true work in life.

My dilemma as a therapist is how to help Dave find the optimum mode of social functioning and contribution, heighten his awareness of his unique personal nature while simultaneously leading him in some way along a spiritual path. Some might say that this is unrealistic or too ambitious a project, that one cannot expect psychotherapy to promote all of these ends, and that one ought to simply delimit the goals of therapy to address one or two of these goals. However, many contemporary individuals who seek psychotherapy have the hope or expectation that it will help them in all three of these areas. The difficulty of this task is insufficient reason for a therapist to shy away from a client's complex and legitimate initiatory longings in the belief that they are asking for too much. Although Dave's difficulties in social adjustment and actualizing his considerable individual potentials appear to have clear roots in childhood trauma that needs to be addressed in his therapy, this is no reason to negate or ignore his genuine striving for spiritual growth and awakening.

While some argue that psychotherapy is a fundamentally different project from traditional spiritual direction or shamanic healing, I agree with Moore that it *functionally* fulfills a similar role in modern, Western culture. To become a true modern rite of passage capable of effecting such complex, multidimensional initiatory passages, psychotherapy needs guiding principles—such as those based on the concept of vocation—that address both the interconnection between, and the potential conflicts that may arise between, the individual, social, and transpersonal levels of initiation.

Dharma, Will, and Transpersonal Activity

Regardless of how we discern the intention of the Guidance Self and an image of our vocation, the experience is typically evident by its deep impact on us. We may sense that something long sought has now been discovered or remembered, or there may be an internal feeling of coming into alignment with our true nature. However, the discovery of a calling is not completed by passively receiving the directives of the Guidance Self. The emergence of an image of our goal, mission, or purpose must meet with our conscious assent and the ability to define and pursue a concrete and specific life task. It is not enough to have a vision or a guiding dream, unless we then redirect the application of our will. Martin

Buber speaks of discovering "the deed that intends me,"[72] and writes,

> Free is the man who wills. . . . He believes in destiny and also that it needs him. . . . He must proceed toward it without knowing where it waits for him. He must go forth with his whole being. . . . He must sacrifice his little will, to his great will to find destiny. Now he no longer interferes, nor does he allow things to happen. He listens to that which grows. . . in order to actualize it in the manner in which it, needing him, wants to be actualized by him—with human spirit and human deed, with human life and human death.[73]

According to Roberto Assagioli, the Self from which one receives directives or images concerning one's vocation, is both passive—a witness, spectator, or observer—and active—a directing agent that intervenes to orchestrate the various functions and energies of the personality.[74] The Self is thus both pure awareness and the source of intention, choice, and will. In his view, the personal will—the capacity for strong and effective choice-making, the capacity to will one's destiny through conscious, deliberate effort—may come into relationship with the "transpersonal will"—a more prescient center of awareness that guides us to act in ways that serve not only our own highest good but also that of others and the world. Reorienting the personal will so that it is responsive to the guidance of the transpersonal will represents a middle way between the emphasis in many systems of Western psychology on strengthening the personal will and the admonition found in many religions to relinquish personal will in order to serve a higher will, "God's will."

Assagioli's theory encompasses both positions, describing a two-way evolutionary path involving the transpersonal will and the conscious personality that may become its agent. Assagioli identifies two main stages in psychological growth: *Personal psychosynthesis* is a process of *individualization* involving the integration of unconscious material and conflicting subpersonalities into a coherent self, with a particular emphasis on training the will, the source of the effective, successful, volitional act[75]; *spiritual psychosynthesis*, on the other hand, involves what Molly Brown[76] calls "superconscious infusion," or what I call the *transpersonalization* of the individual. It entails the revelation of impulses, archetypal images, or sense of purpose having their origins in the transpersonal Self.

Transpersonalization occurs through two means: disidentification of the personal self from egoic drives and motives, and the subsequent "dedication of the personal will to the spiritual will"; or, alternatively, "the spiritual will, the spiritual Self, takes possession of and utilizes the personal will." [77] Either way, in transpersonalization our personal will, efforts, and aspirations are felt to be aligned with some larger field of activity—whether we define this as the intentions of the Guidance Self, the will of God, or, as Dane Rudhyar[78] suggests, the needs of some portion of humanity at a given time and place—a collective purpose for whose fulfillment an agent is needed.

Rudhyar calls the agent of such transpersonal activity a "transpersonal individual," one possessing stable personal boundaries, clarity of mind, creative skills, *and* self-consecration to, and readiness to serve, the transpersonal will. A transpersonal individual engages in skillful willed acts that are called forth by, and responsive to, a collective need, the condition of a larger network of beings in which the individual is a participant.[79]

> The whole situation involves a definite spiritual Quality seeking precise and concrete actualization in a differentiated form (a person) . . . , according to a fundamental archetypal structure. . . . Transpersonal activity implies a definite interaction between the performer of the transpersonal act and its spiritual source transcending the strictly human level of consciousness. . . . The human receiver acts as a focalizing agent for the need of his people and his culture.[80]

Rudhyar emphasizes that a transpersonal individual's actions may be inspired by motives other than the achievement of socially defined success.[81] The pursuit of our personal calling, or svadharma, may at times be at odds with our cultural dharma, bringing us into conflict with cultural norms, values, and expectations and disrupting our social functioning or sense of personal certitude or contentment. But such crises are, in his view, occasions for transmuting karma—our culturally and historically determined circumstances—into dharma, a sacred performance of the purpose with which, he says, each of us was invested at birth.[82]

For Rudhyar, dharma is a form of transpersonal activity that implies more than just a search for altered states of consciousness and personal enlightenment; rather, it is a dynamic concept referring to spiritually inspired actions performed with a transformative, catalytic intent. Such creative actions are what enable us to make a creative response to our given conditions, thereby fulfilling not only our individual calling, but also our place in both culture and the cosmos. When a vocation is expressed as a form of transpersonal activity, the universal, social, and individual dimensions of vocation, while at times in conflict, are ultimately interconnected. A calling is a life task that enables us to fulfill, in an individually appropriate manner, our place in the universal order.

6

Inflation: The Shadow of Vocation

Thus far, I have emphasized the positive ways in which a vocation enables us to organize our identity and efforts around a central life project. However, it seems appropriate here to offer some thoughts about the dark side of a sense of vocation—the problem of inflation or grandiosity. For example, how can we distinguish between the healthy need each person has to define a vocation and an inflated expression of one's sense of calling—which may lead to interpersonal difficulties or problems in social adjustment, or which may be a sign of serious mental disorder? Moreover, it is important not to forget that wars have been fought because one person's or one nation's sense of vocation conflicted with that of another. Philosopher Donald Rothberg has noted that this raises complex ethical questions concerning how one is to judge whether or not a particular person's or nation's sense of vocation—for example, the strong sense of vocation of Hitler and German Nazis—is dangerous and to be rejected.[83]

Inflation results from taking one's personal myth and its narrative of life purpose too seriously—to the point of megalomania, the belief in some extraordinary personal mission. Jung believed this may result from an unwise or uncontrolled immersion in unconscious realms leading to a potentially dangerous *identification* with archetypal material.[84]

Indeed this pattern of inflation and grandiosity is a central part of the phenomenology of psychosis. According to psychiatrist John Weir Perry, schizophrenia often entails a spontaneous reappearance of the ancient mythology of kingship, which he views as an attempt to reestablish an internal center of order to counteract the fragmented, chaotic condition of the psychotic state.[85] The constellation of the kingship archetype allows one who has been an outsider, a person with "a markedly damaged self-image" who feels powerless and ineffectual, to compensate by activating "the archetypes of supreme power to order, direct and structure the psychic life." [86] As participants in "a ritual drama emerging spontaneously from the psychic depth," psychotic individuals experience images that are symbols for the kingly functions of "self assertion, mastery, and purposeful aggression, all that goes into establishing an effective ego consciousness in a societal context." [87]

According to Perry, the role of the sacral king evolved historically into that of the messianic hero. In psychosis, this role takes the form of ideas of supreme rule, the urgent belief in one's *messianic calling* to save the world or redeem society— usually in the context of imagery of an apocalyptic battle between the forces of light and dark or good and evil that climaxes with the individual being raised up to "a position of world rulership or spiritual leadership." [88] The emergence of images of the messianic, redeeming hero may also take the form of an inflation, the direct identification with the image.

Thus, Perry cautions, "The image should be taken as a source of energy, not a description of one's ego." [89]

Gary Rosenthal views inflation as part of the natural process of spiritual or transpersonal development.[90] He identifies five factors supporting the formation or "crystallization" of inflation: characterological predispos-itions, psychological disruption by spiritual experiences, egoic appropriation of spiritual experiences, external reinforcement of grandiosity by a group or leader, and the absence or dismissal of disconfirming feedback. The inflated system may be dispersed or "decrystallized" by penetration of the inflated self-sense by disconfirming feedback, realization of the distortion of one's inflated actions and attitudes, and a return to "beginner's mind," enabling one to "assimilate transpersonal dimensions of experience without activating the ego into inflation." [91]

Issues of vocation and inflation can be central to psychotherapeutic work. Stephen Johnson has noted that individuals exhibiting a narcissistic personality structure have developed a grandiose self to compensate for the repeated injury caused by not having the real, authentic self validated, accepted, and loved by parental figures.[92] The psychotherapy of the narcissistic adult, in his view, centers around uncovering the unrealistic goals and self-image of the grandiose self; containing the underlying depression and sense of worthlessness and depletion that emerge when the grandiose self's strivings and expectations of perfection inevitably fail; gradually developing a set of realistic, attainable goals and ambitions; and building stable self-esteem through real, enduring accomplishments. This, in short, describes the transformation of inflation into vocation.

To sum up, initiation into a calling or a vocation may sometimes involve a form of inflation, which can either lead to the pitfalls that Rosenthal identifies or to the constitution of the energy and dynamism of the self that Perry describes. I believe that when gradually decrystallized and purified of grandiosity and messianism, a sense of vocation can become a source of inspired, sustained efforts to carry out the vocational task in the social world.

The discovery of a personal calling is often accompanied by the emergence in dreams or imagination of an archetypal figure, such as that of shaman, guru, or healer. One can literalize this, becoming inflated and overly identified with these figures, and making statements regarding one's personal mission that others might view as inappropriate. Or this archetypal "infusion" might motivate the individual to take concrete strides toward expressing the vocation in the world in a grounded, culturally appropriate way. Indeed, it is often the ethical standards of a given community that define in many instances whether a given person's calling is considered a true and valid vocation or not. The often difficult struggle to bring one's individual sense of calling within the philosophical, ideological, and behavioral parameters deemed acceptable by one's culture is the source of the moral tension implicit in the pursuit of vocation.

We have seen that dharma or personal vocation is central to our understanding of a number of other important topics, such as initiation, dreams, inner voices, synchronicity, and individuation. Vocation provides a bridge between apprehension of transcendent, transpersonal, or spiritual dimensions of life in states of expanded consciousness and meaningful, purposeful action in the world. I have touched on the possibility that one's own sense of calling may conflict with social norms in some manner, an experience that often requires significant moral choices and acts of personal courage. I have also briefly commented on the dark side of vocation, and suggested that an alertness to the potential for inflation is an important part of defining a mature sense of vocation.

Now let us turn our attention to some basic principles that can help us move toward the attainment our calling—that inspiring image of our potential destination that reveals itself in so many ways when our hearts and minds are attentive.

PART II

Eight Steps to

Finding Your Life's Calling

7

Introduction to Part II: Vocation as a Personal Narrative

One of the best ways to learn anything is to listen to other people's stories. To learn more about finding a calling, I interviewed a number of people, asking them to tell me how they discovered their vocations and what impact these experiences had on their lives. In the chapters that follow I will quote excerpts from some of their stories to illuminate our discussion.

To understand how a calling contributes to the unfolding story of an individual's life, let us briefly consider some ideas about the role of narrative in human existence. Psychologist Donald Polkinghorne writes,

> Narrative is one of the forms of expressiveness through which life events are conjoined into coherent, meaningful, unified themes. . . . [A narrative is] a linked series of episodes contributing to a single adventure with a beginning, middle, and an end. . . . We achieve our personal identity and self concept through the use of the narrative configuration, and make our existence into a whole by understanding it as an expression of a single unfolding and developing story. . . . The self is that temporal order of human existence whose story

begins with birth, has as its middle the episodes of a life span, and ends with death. It is the plot that gathers together these events into a coherent and meaningful unity, and thereby gives context and significance to the contribution that individual episodes make toward the overall configuration that is the person. [93]

The centrality of vocation to our evolving identities has been illuminated by Donald McAdams, who views identity as a process of forging unity and purpose out of our lives through "binding together of past, present, and future." [94] He writes,

Identity is a life story. . . . The problem of identity is the problem of arriving at a life story that provides unity and purpose— within a socio-historical matrix that embodies a much larger story. . . . The story provides a coherent narrative framework within which the disparate events and the various roles of a person's life can be embedded and given meaning.... [Human beings are] organisms who, in their quest for identity, are impelled by the desire to construct their own biographies. [95]

McAdams views identity as a narrative construction or life story organized around two central motivations: the *power* and *intimacy* motives. The power motive refers to the desire to be potent, powerful, and effective and often appears in images of strength, status, or triumph over the physical environment, others, destiny, or oneself. The intimacy motive is concerned with relationship and intimacy with others, and emerges in images of community, friendship, or love.

A significant feature of life stories are *nuclear episodes*, "significant life episodes that, in the narrating mind of the individual, are reconstructed to fit into the life story as its most significant scenes." [96] These are "seen by the individual reconstructing his or her past as turning points marking the end of one chapter and the beginning of another." [97] Nuclear episodes may include earliest memories, nadir experiences (reaching bottom, low points in life), and peak experiences, "personal episodes of perceived wholeness, ego transcendence, truth and goodness, heightened sensation, pure delight, completion, innocence and so forth." [98] McAdams notes an important distinction between nuclear *episodes of continuity*, which "reinforce the sameness of identity over time", and *episodes of transformation*, which "mark relatively discontinuous changes in the life story." [99] Episodes of transformation may function as "identity or origin myths, detailing the genesis of a particular value or value system. . . [or] perceived personal trait." [100]

McAdams's ideas contribute significantly to our understanding of vocation. As the examples will illustrate, finding a calling often helps us bind together our past, present, and future, and thus plays a central role in the construction of our personal life stories. We will also note that, to the extent that defining and pursuing a central project enables us to feel both personally effective and significantly related to others, vocation is a means of fulfilling our drives for both power and intimacy. In addition, the following accounts illustrate that finding a vocation is an important kind of nuclear episode that must be meaningfully situated within a person's larger life story. In Part I we saw that a calling often emerges through initiatory events or mystical experiences that take the form of a revelation of individual purpose. We will see below that such initiations may function either as episodes of continuity or episodes of transformation.

The stories cited in these chapters are rich in insights and suggestive images. You will meet a number of people who have found their callings in a variety of ways. As you read their accounts a number of contrasts and dichotomies between them will become apparent. In some cases the individual's vocation is closely related to his or her profession or career, whereas in other cases it refers solely to a personally meaningful activity or objective unrelated to the person's means of livelihood. While some describe feeling special or receiving positive attention from others as a result of finding their calling, others report a sense of isolation or stigmatization. Some say that a sense of vocation has helped their lives "come together" and has integrated their prior interests, while others report that their lives "fell apart" as a consequence of the vocation or that the initiatory experience overturned their prior interests and goals. Their accounts reveal that discovering a calling can be a one-time event or a gradual, evolving process. Vocation can be actively sought or the experience can occur spontaneously and take one completely by surprise. A calling can involve either a tradition-bound or tradition-breaking path.

Most importantly, the stories of these individuals illustrate the eight steps of finding a life's calling.

- 1. Preparation to find a vocation.
- 2. Experiencing illumination.
- 3. Receiving confirmation of the calling.
- 4. Development of our skill in the vocation.
- 5. Coping with interpersonal issues and searching for a shared sense of calling.
- 6. Resolving problems and pitfalls.

- 7. Building a sacred vessel so that vocation becomes a spiritual path.
- 8. Defining the meaning of a calling.

These eight steps do not necessarily unfold in a particular, sequential order and thus should not be viewed as a linear map of the journey. Rather, these are eight steps that most people go through at some point—often concurrently— on the path of following a vocation. I hope that the stories illustrating these eight steps will enable you to see more clearly how to find, pursue, and find fulfillment in your own life's calling.

8

Preparation

To find our calling, we need to prepare ourselves, to make ourselves ready. Not everyone finds a calling during his or her lifetime, and those people who do often pass through significant periods of searching and questing before they achieve illumination of their life's central work. I have identified three major facets of preparation for the vocation: completion, internal preparation, and deconditioning.

Completion

Completion begins with the awareness that one period of life is ending and a new phase has yet to begin. At times this is associated with a feeling of emptiness or of not being fulfilled, or a recognition that we're looking for something new in our lives. Completion might mean leaving a relationship or a job, or finishing up some prior commitment. It may also involve letting go of inauthentic activities, pursuits we no longer find fulfilling. For example, if spending hours watching TV and drinking beer every night no longer nourishes us, we might not be certain of what else to do, but it might be a good idea to start by turning off the tube and sitting in meditation or reading a good book.

To better understand the stage of completion, let's consider the example of John, a thirty-nine-year-old environmental activist, a landscape gardener, and a student of the new field of deep ecology. He also writes articles on environmental issues for his local newspaper.

> I started out in life pursuing a conventional career. I tried law school but dropped out, much to the chagrin of my father. Then my dad helped me get me a job as a stockbroker in a large New York firm. I did that for two years. I had money, a nice car, stocks, prestige, and a glamorous job that really impressed people, especially women. But I began to feel that something wasn't right. My life felt empty. Everyone in the corporate world seemed so greedy and materialistic. One day, after I had been reading about the prevalence of hunger and homelessness in our society, I had lunch with a colleague who struck me as hideous, greedy, and gluttonous—he kept talking about his trips to Bermuda and Thailand, his golf game, and his expensive computer system. The contrast of his lifestyle, and my own, with the neediness of others really struck me. And I thought to myself, "I don't want to live like this." After that, I went into a deep depression, which my therapist tried to convince me was a result of my unhappy childhood, and a fear of success in the business world. This seemed totally inaccurate to me, for I sensed that I was depressed because something was fundamentally wrong about the whole way I was living.

As we will see later, John underwent a fierce internal struggle that ultimately led him to let go of a career that provided him with considerable prestige and material success but that seemed fundamentally inauthentic. His account suggests that a major prerequisite to initiation into a sense of vocation is knowing what one does *not* wish to be or become. His recognition that money was no longer in itself a primary source of value or meaning prepared him to find a more enduring set of values and priorities, eventually leading him to discover his true vocation as an environmental activist. Recognizing the emptiness of a predominantly materialistic way of life, John began to let go of the old self. He relinquished the job his father had helped him get, and a very solid salary. But it wasn't enough for him. This disillusionment helped prepare him to find his true vocation.

Another aspect of completion occurs when things begin to change in ways we do not consciously intend or desire and in ways that require that we look to the future. Recently I counseled a man whose career of twenty years had crumbled completely. No matter how hard he tried, he could no longer get hired in his field. After he got over his initial panic about possibly ending up on the streets, homeless, he realized that the cycle of his involvement in that field was completing itself so he could move on to something else. He quieted himself down through meditation and kept listening.

One day he called to tell me he had figured out what he wanted to do: He was going to start a business of his own. "I always knew I'd do this one day," he said. "But I was so busy with my career that I forgot." This man was able to accept change and to view his career transition as a process of completion rather than a tragic, purposeless setback. His story also illustrates the importance of centering yourself so that you can listen to your heart. This brings us to the next stage of preparation.

Internal Preparation

Internal preparation involves making ourselves inwardly ready to receive illumination of our direction. As we have just seen, an important facet of internal preparation is centering or quieting ourselves down so we can hear our inner voice and discern what is really calling to us from inside. Some religious traditions speak of the need to empty ourselves and calm our minds so that we might hear the voice of God. Thus, meditation and prayer are often helpful. Resolution of lingering emotional issues such as a fear of failure is another example of internal preparation. Changing one's attitude about work, money, ambition, and other issues may also be a prerequisite to effective work in the vocation. We may also need to learn to forgive others and clear up old interpersonal problems that create fear, resentment, agitation, and disturbance of mind. Practicing yoga, gardening, and taking long walks are just a few examples of other ways to bring yourself into balance during the stage of preparation.

In addition, suffering is often a facet of internal preparation, because through suffering we learn courage, our hearts open, and we come closer to our own pain and the pain of others. For example, Pat, a forty-two-year-old woman who practices Chinese medicine, acupuncture, and herbology, reported the following:

> Before I found my path I was guided by an inner voice to clear up my relationship with my parents so that I would be free to leave my home town and never return. I was also told that I would eventually live in California. I later had a precognitive dream of my husband's death. I was informed that the loss of my husband was a sacrifice that would prepare me for doing

the work that was meant for me. This dream revealed that all was as it should be, that there is an intelligent order in life, and that all experiences are teachings. Later, I came to understand that my vocation as a doctor requires wisdom about death and impermanence, and that the death of my husband gave me the courage to deal with any situation that could possibly arise with a patient and know that I could handle it.

Note that Pat's inner guidance to complete old business and interpersonal commitments before she was guided to a new task in life illustrates the process of completion described above. She also viewed her suffering after her husband's death as an essential lesson that prepared her internally for her role as a physician.

Deconditioning

Deconditioning involves liberating yourself from societal norms, from internalized parental voices, from traditional religious beliefs and doctrines, or from other people's expectations in order to pursue your individual calling. If your parents always taught you that you ought to get married and start having children in your early twenties, you may pass through some inner conflict if you decide to take a different course in life—perhaps deciding to return to school or become a sculptor or sail around the world. Perhaps you realize that marriage and having children is not your primary goal or priority—at least during this stage of your life. No one else can tell you what your calling should be. To find out what we want to do with our lives, we have to decondition ourselves from old beliefs, dogmas, and parental conditioning.

Jill, a very talented, creative artist struggling to reconcile her desire for stability and conformity to family expectations with the pursuit of her creative strivings, had the following dream:

> I am in New York. I am supposed to meet my father for lunch downtown in a diner by the bridge. I go to the one he suggests. This is a long, crowded, old chrome diner. It's noisy and wet. I go next door to another restaurant and get a table there. My father comes and joins me there.
>
> Then I'm in another time and place. I am in Jamaica. I'm free. I feel good. I belong here. I am happy, dancing and walking through a beachy field. I have a drum. I go to where several musicians have gathered and I play. They don't mind, and I feel confident. Weekly practice has paid off, and I know how to keep a beat. My drum is different from any I've ever played. I am a newcomer, but they welcome me.
>
> Then I'm at the office where I work. I'm thinking about the drum, and all I want to do is practice. I look over at the printer and notice that it's all out of paper. Then I notice that over to one side there are piles of different kinds of odd-sized paper. It's 15 x 14, 11 x 12, 8 x 9, really nice. I want it for stationery. It's got texture. It's beautiful—earth tones, soft, old-fashioned. I look over and see that my boss has thrown it out. So I retrieve as much of it as I can.

Jill stated that the Jamaica scene reminded her of the Jamaican Rastafarian metaphor of Babylon—referring to the materialistic world exemplified by cities like New York. For her, Babylon represents having a steady job in an office, reporting to her parents about her activities, the old world she would like to leave behind. In contrast, Jamaica symbolizes the place where she finds her own song, her own vision, her own rhythm, her own voice. It is a place of possibility, where youthful, idealistic dreams of freedom, of creativity, and of forming a new society have not died. In her associations to this dream, Jill felt that it symbolized an internal conflict between staying bound to the lifestyle and activities that would be acceptable to her parents (going to the diner her father recommends) and pursuing a path of freedom and creativity (going to the other restaurant, wanting a different menu of life choices).

Jill found something valuable onto which she wanted to place her own mark or stamp (the stationery), and it was based on something odd shaped, unusual, atypical. Jill felt that this dream indicated that she had already made a choice, an irrevocable decision to be free. The dream helped her hold within her awareness the fact that she lives in two worlds, the world of her father and the world of the musicians, dancers, and creative people. She visits both in the dream, indicating her need to validate both parts of her life. "I am Babylon *and* I am Jamaica," she said, summing up the meaning of this dream—which beautifully portrays the process of deconditioning, of letting of images, thoughts, or constructs defining who you are supposed to be so that you can determine who you are and who you want to become.

In the stage of preparation it's important for us to learn to trust that we will be guided, and that we will find the appropriate form to express our essential nature in the world. To complete and let go of the past, decondition ourselves, and prepare ourselves internally for the illumination of purpose to occur, we often have to make radical choices and put ourselves in unusual circumstances. Sometimes we have to rip ourselves away from everything known and familiar even though we don't know what we're looking for.

Earlier, I spoke of the need for self-created rites of initiation. Very often today we must provide our own support system and consecrate a certain place and period of time to the search for direction, meaning, a sense of what path to follow. The results are often not sudden or dramatic. Lightning bolts don't usually strike, nor do most people hear voices or see florid visions. Rather, we may simply feel drawn in a particular direction, to a new interest or pursuit. Insight often emerges in the form of a fantasy, an idea, or an interest in a particular book, class, or workshop.

The essence of the stage of preparation to discover a calling is to empty ourselves and search or pray for a vision. Listening to our dreams is one way we can prepare ourselves to receive inner guidance. Also, in many cases it is very useful to ritualize our quest in some way. In our current cultural environment many people find that they need to deliberately create an environment in which they can search for illumination. Let me briefly tell you about my own period of preparation.

My Story

At the beginning of this book I described how I became focused on inner growth early in my life, and how I felt that my calling was to be a spiritual practitioner. I spent years studying yoga and meditation with various teachers, and I even traveled to India, where a period of intense spiritual searching and realization still left me deeply uncertain about my ultimate direction. At that time I was what I call a premature mystic, experiencing states of consciousness that were quite extraordinary but with no way of anchoring these in ordinary life. I entered a new phase of my spiritual journey when I realized that I was going to have to translate my spirituality into a path in the world.

However, when I graduated from college I had absolutely no idea what I wanted to do or how I would make my way. I was interested in poetry and music but didn't have a clue about how to translate those interests into a livelihood. I needed some time to find myself and intuitively sensed that the best way to do this was to travel, but before I could do this I would need to save some money. So I found a job as a proofreader, saved up some cash, and daydreamed about the future adventures I might have. I felt a pull away from familiar places and activities and toward the unknown. I was ready for a rite of passage that the intellectual rigors of college had not adequately provided. Lacking a container for ritual initiation, I had to create and embark upon my own vision quest.

One day I bought a one-way ticket out of New York City and boarded a bus to Colorado with a backpack stuffed full of my worldly possessions. I had vague ideas of pursuing a career out West as a musician. But in truth, my actual destination was unknown. I was leaving not only my family, the city where I had grown up, and my friends, but also a spiritual community with which I'd been affiliated for many years. Although I had no idea where I was going, I knew I was on a quest to find my path in life.

I spent months wandering all over the Southwest and Pacific Northwest with no specific destination. I hitchhiked around, slept in a tent in the woods, and spent most of my time outdoors meditating, fasting, praying for guidance, reading, observing and listening to nature, writing in my journal, and waiting for inspiration.

Instead of going straight from college to a job, I appeared to many people to be headed straight into the gutter. No one could understand what I was doing. But I knew intuitively that I had to be "melted down" before I could find my direction. That meant allowing myself to be completely lost in the woods and to let go of trying to please my parents. I felt that I was following Ariadne's thread into a labyrinth of mystery where I knew, when I finally reached the center, I would find a new clarity about my direction.

I used to physically enact a ritual in which I would create a medicine wheel, placing stones on the ground out in the forest, with one stone in the center. Constructing such a wheel was a ceremonial process of casting a circle and creating symbolic order in the center of my own chaos. The circle represents wholeness and order. I wasn't thinking to myself "I'm creating order and wholeness." I just did this spontaneously, because intuitively it felt good. Then I'd walk around the medicine wheel in a meditative frame of mind, pointing one hand and focusing my gaze on the center of the circle. As I did this, I meditated on the idea that at the center of my being was the answer that I sought and that I was being guided to my task, my work in life.

I ritualized my search in this manner, calling to my invisible spiritual guides, asking to be shown the way. I circumambulated the as-yet unrevealed secret of my own nature and my life's path, witnessing each footstep as necessary, even these seemingly aimless ones. Thus, I passed through an extended period of formlessness before a new identity took shape. Eventually I began to perceive an image of myself as a writer, teacher, and spiritual counselor. Gradually I would begin to mold myself into this image.

I am not suggesting that such a period of external wandering and internal uncertainty is necessary for everyone. However, many people do find that they must in some way die to the old self and the old life, remaining temporarily formless, before assuming the new form of their life's calling. This is the just the way preparation unfolded for me. Regardless of the form preparation takes, however, I believe that in many instances a necessary prerequisite to the discovery of a life's calling is a period of questioning and searching, often requiring that we relinquish an old identity or life structure, and put aside familiar activities.

Of course, the danger is of wandering, searching, and staying unfocused indefinitely or even permanently, which is not a desirable situation. I know a number of people in their forties or fifties who are still confused about who they are and unable to make any decisions. The point is to recognize that such a period of confusion and searching is a phase that must then be followed by other phases of personal evolution in which there is a deep clarity about one's purpose and the steps needed to make it real.

Steps for Preparation

If we circumambulate the center of our own beings reverently and receptively, and consciously live through our periods of searching and preparation fully, eventually clarity emerges. Some interior part of ourselves knows what's right for us. Preparation means creating room in our lives for that internal guidance to reveal itself and show us the way. This means creating a special environment or time set apart for inner emptying of ourselves, for inner listening. What is required during the stage of preparation is longing, a clarity of intention to find our life's work.

If you sincerely want to find your life's calling, try pursuing some of the following suggestions.

Go on a Vision Quest.

You don't need to spend thousands of dollars, nor do you need to fast until you are near death while you pray for a vision. Just go camping or stay in a house or cabin in a quiet, secluded place for several days. Eat lightly, or fast responsibly. Avoid distractions (TV, radio, books read for mere diversion). Spend your time meditating, praying, writing in your journal, playing music, and being close to nature. Witness the beauty that surrounds you, and listen to the wind, birds singing, and the rustling of leaves. Most of all, listen to your heart. What is it saying to you? If you listen within, you will find your answers.

You can create your vision quest in any way you choose. You can do it by going into retreat in the desert or by spending some quiet time alone in your own home. You are more likely to figure out what you want to do in a setting consecrated to that purpose. Ritualize the quest. Invent your own ceremony. Initiate yourself.

I did a very radical thing. I checked out of society for over a year. I allowed myself the opportunity to be totally confused. In some ways, however, my circumstances were unusual. I had several thousand dollars saved up to live on, and I had no responsibilities to others at that stage in my life. It is harder to take time off once you have a spouse, children, a mortgage, a business to run, or aging parents or ailing relatives to care for.

Nevertheless, I know many people who have successfully quested on weekends, or taking a week off from work to go on a trip. If you have the longing, you can find the time and resources to search for your calling.

Incubate a Dream.

Another way of ritualizing one's search for a calling is dream incubation, which can be extremely powerful. To do this, repeat the following procedure until you receive the answers you are looking for. Before retiring at night, spend some time thinking about your quest for a sacred personal path, a life's calling. Ask the Guidance Self within you for assistance in the dream state. Think intensely about your questions, about your dilemma, about what you are longing for, and about how you want things to change. Ask your unconscious for clarity and insight, for an answer to your questions. Affirm to yourself that you will receive guidance while you sleep, and affirm that you will remember your dreams and write them down upon awakening; even the smallest dream fragment can be valuable. Sustain this practice until a dream comes. It won't necessarily happen the first night.

There are literally dozens of fantastic books on the market to help you understand your dreams. Two that I especially like are *Dreamtime and Dreamwork* by Stanley Krippner, and *The Jungian-Senoi Dreamwork Manual* by Strephon Kaplan Williams.

Consult With an Astrologer.

A good astrologer can help you understand your essential identity and what your most appropriate next steps are—whether that means to study and establish your credentials, to earn more money, to explore your creativity, or to find more fulfillment in relationships. I know many people who have gained important insights into their vocational potentials and goals after having a birth chart reading. A skillful reading can greatly change your direction and perception of possible options. One woman I know, a dancer who had been injured and thus needed to make a new start, consulted with an astrologer about her career potentials. She was completely taken by surprise when the astrologer told her that she would make a great lawyer. After she recovered from her initial shock, she realized that this idea intrigued her, that she had never even imagined such a career before but that it made sense to her. She began to pursue this new goal, challenging herself to return to school where she studied new subjects like ethics, political science, and environmental science in preparation for her new profession. Very different priorities emerged for her, new activities ensued, and she began to form a new identity.

Astrology is often viewed with skepticism in our culture because it does not seem to operate according to the accepted laws of science. However, those who discount the validity of this form of perennial wisdom often do so without properly and objectively investigating the topic. Astrology is a contemplative discipline, a language of symbols that reveals sacred knowledge about the cycles of life. The banal predictions found in newspaper Sun-sign columns are *not* real astrology—which requires careful study of an accurately calculated chart of all the major planets (not just the Sun) at the place and time of a person's birth. People around the world continue to study the celestial art because it helps them guide themselves through life with wisdom and clarity. Of course, to utilize astrology properly, a non-deterministic attitude is best. The planets don't *make* things happen to us. Rather, astrologers view the planets as *symbols* of various kinds of human experiences and their probable timing.

Pay Attention to Your Heart's Longings and Your Mind's Interests.

What are you longing to do? Where are you yearning to be? If you could do whatever you wanted, what would you do? Project into the future and ask yourself who you would like to be in two years, five years, and ten years. Take note of your heart's true inclinations. The small fantasy or image you have now may be a vibrant seed that will one day grow into the tree of your life's work.

Earn and Save Money So You Can Travel and Search.

Have some fuel in your pocket so that once you figure out what you want to do you can go for it! It can be extremely useful to have some savings so you can afford to take seminars or classes or travel as part of a personal quest. I was fortunate that I had enough money saved that I could travel for a period of time. But even if you don't have much money, you can still search and move toward achieving your vocation.

Regardless of your circumstances, humble or opulent, the key to preparation is consecrating a particular place and period of your life for this purpose only, to find the answer to these questions: Who am I to become? What am I to do? What is my calling? Which path do I wish to take? Do not be discouraged if your search does not yield immediate results. The answers will come in time. You have to be consistent, you have to sustain your efforts, and you have to focus. Simply put, there's often an incubation period involved in finding your life's calling.

9

Illumination

Preparation is a clearing of the ground so that illumination of our calling in life becomes possible. In moments of illumination we realize the nature of our personal vocation. This can occur in a variety of settings. As noted in Part I, many people discover a sense of vocation in fairly dramatic ways through sensing an inner voice, visions, dreams, near-death experiences, shamanic journeys, deep meditation, and use of oracular methods. For others, illumination occurs more subtly, through an inner knowing or certainty, spontaneous insights and realizations, a sense of inner peace, a sense that "it fits," feeling "in tune," or a sense of "rightness." In some instances, a teacher's influence is central. Other common contexts for illumination include receiving positive feedback from others; being inspired by a book, a lecture, or the example of others; religious conversion; receiving initiation into a technique of inner growth like meditation; and having a curiosity about a particular kind of work. Many people report gaining insight about their direction while traveling. For example, a woman I know received guidance to move in a new direction in her life while in the presence of a Tibetan trance oracle. Travel to sacred places can often bring great inspiration. In many instances our life purpose comes into clear focus once we are removed from the setting of our everyday routines and have the chance to clear ourselves and listen.

Another frequently mentioned setting for illumination is childhood premonitions. For example, let us look at the example of a thirty-three-year-old woman named Jan who paints portraits that attempt to capture the spiritual essence of a person and their destiny in life. She reports,

> I had childhood glimmerings and premonitions of my calling through a natural affinity for art and intuitive insights into others. When I was a child I also had visions of a spirit being that awakened in me an interest in nonphysical realms of existence. These experiences led to questioning and searching for my life purpose, and eventually gave rise to spontaneous knowing that I possessed a unique gift and talent. I had remarkable skill in painting from the very beginning, as if I was remembering how to do this work from a prior lifetime. Subsequently this was confirmed by a psychic, and during a session of past-life recall. I also received recognition of my gift from elders, teachers, and peers. For example, in the first painting class I ever took, I felt like I knew instinctively how to paint before I really knew anything about it. Soon I was expressing my intuitions about people through my art.
>
> When I found my work as painter I felt like I was a natural at it. It came easily to me and it fit my personality. However, I have also felt isolated at times because of my calling, as if I was different from others. However, I know I have found my work in life because when I do it I feel in tune with everything, knowing I am where I belong. Whenever I do a painting, I get a feeling of exhilaration that I have not found doing anything else.

Another person who had a childhood awakening to a calling is Ralph, a forty-six-year-old man who works as an organizational consultant.

> As a child I had a psychic gift: I had visions of scenes from my older relatives' lives, of things that happened to them as children that they'd never told me, for example. And they would confirm the accuracy of what I'd seen. One of my uncles encouraged me to develop my intuition, and I began answering questions that people would ask me. I had a high level of accuracy about people's problems. This was between ages five and ten.

Illumination as a Peak or Nadir Experience

Illumination of one's vocation is often associated with positive peak experiences. For example, let us consider the example of Judy, a freelance writer in her mid-forties who specializes in articles on TV, film, and literary criticism, and in experimental forms of fiction.

> I discovered my calling in life when I was in second grade. My teacher was reading to us from a Dr. Seuss book called *On Beyond Zebra*, which is about an alphabet that extends beyond the letter "Z." As she read this, I felt an energetic sensation of tingling up my spine and a state of bliss, joy, and possibility. My teacher noticed that something had happened to me and gave me the book afterward. This story made me realize in an instant that my work in life is to live in a world beyond rules and parameters, beyond language and an alphabet that's been given, and to teach others that we can make things up—and that there's more to life than what we are given. I felt special, chosen, and blessed because of this experience, as if I had been

singled out. This experience foreshadowed my later work as a creative writer. My vocation is the freedom to create my own reality, and it was revealed to me through walking into another world of perception and possibility when I was seven years old.

However, illumination of a calling may also stem from *nadir* experiences, what in common parlance are known as "downers" or "bummers." Ralph, the man who had psychic and healing gifts from his childhood reports the following:

When I was ten I had a dream that my father died, including many details about the exact circumstances of his death. A year later he actually did die, precisely as I had dreamt about it. That event shook me up tremendously because I thought maybe I had caused his death. Whereas earlier I'd seen myself as special and a little bit superior to others, my father's death really shattered me and made me view my psychic gift as an awful thing. I thought that if I'd done something differently maybe he wouldn't have died. So I shut down my psychic gifts for the most part, although at times I realized that I still had clear access to other people's thoughts.

An example of a calling that emerged out of a peak experience followed by a nadir experience is John, the man we discussed earlier who started out as a stockbroker until he began to question his way of life. As he reports it, during a period of deep depression and uncertainty,

I went on a camping trip in Montana that changed my life. I perceived the radiance, intelligence, aliveness, and consciousness of the trees, and the incredible beauty of wild animals like birds, foxes, raccoons, and deer. It was the first time I had been out in nature for a long time, and the first time I had felt so relaxed, happy, and at peace since I was a boy. And I began to wonder, how can I go back to New York?

One night, lying on a hillside looking at the sky, I felt the stars above me and the Earth below me breathing. I felt how my own life was connected to this much greater life, the great pulse of creation. In all directions I was surrounded by conscious light and life. This was the closest to a religious experience I've ever had, a moment of epiphany like the ones romantic poets like Wordsworth described. I was just a molecule in this vast universe. I thought of New York again and said to myself, "I do not want to go back to that." I asked myself why didn't I just leave. But then I thought to myself kind of cynically, "Yeah, and do what?" Then I heard an inner voice say to me very softly, "The Mother will take care of you." I wondered if I was crazy and went to sleep and tried to forget about this whole episode.

I went back to New York and began hating my job even more. I tried to buckle down and keep going, even though I hated this way of life. Then, about five weeks later, I remembered the experience on the hillside, the inner voice, and the peace I had known in nature. And I thought, "This is it. I'm leaving. I'm going back to nature. I don't know where I'm going, but I gotta get out of here. This is killing me." And I did it. I quit my job, took an exploratory trip to Portland, came back to New York, sold some of my belongings, and drove a U-Haul truck back to Portland. I had no idea what I was going to do. But I knew this was the most important decision of my life, and that I had to cut myself loose of everything back there before I would discover whatever else I might do—to make myself available for something else to happen, whatever it might be.

Then one day hiking in the Cascades, I saw a huge area of forest that had been clear-cut. It was a hideous sight, like a hellish graveyard, and I felt how the spirits of the ancient trees that had lived there for centuries had been hurt. It made me so angry that I cried. All those trees had been killed just to serve human needs for wood and paper. I realized that it wasn't right, that the trees have as much right to be here as we do, and that cutting them down was no different that an act of cold-hearted murder carried out without gratitude or reverence. It was a total waste of a natural resource that has incalculable value and beauty in its own right.

That experience awakened me to environmental issues and got me involved in efforts to stop the destruction of the planet. I read books on ecology and green politics, attended meetings of environmental and antinuclear groups, and participated in various demonstrations. I'm quite active now in the ecology movement and other efforts to promote a more sustainable way of life.

Illumination as Nuclear Episode: Continuity and Transformation of Identity

Moments of illumination such as those we have just examined are what Donald McAdams calls the "nuclear episodes" of vocation. Illumination of a calling may be either an episode of continuity or an episode of transformation in McAdams's sense, with a greater weight in the direction of episodes of transformation. In some instances vocation provides an integration of prior goals and interests, and the binding together of the person's past, present, and future in a way that preserves the essential continuity of the individual's identity. Upon moving to California, Pat, the acupuncturist, stated that,

I met a teacher of Chinese medicine I was immediately drawn to, who accepted me as a personal apprentice and student. I found that this new interest immediately captivated me, and I knew with complete certainty that this was my vocation. I found that the philosophy and practice of Chinese medicine was the perfect integration of my interests and the way of life that I had been seeking, especially with respect to the balance of the four elements of nature.

Yet, in contrast, other people find that discovery of a vocation involves a transformation of identity that often occurs only after one relinquishes an old self-image, career, goal, world view, or relationship. For example, John was transformed from an ambitious, materialistic stockbroker into an environmentalist-activist living according to entirely new priorities. Another story that illustrates a major transformation of identity is that of Donna, a woman in her mid-fifties who has been a nun for over thirty years. For Donna, the calling to become a nun created a radical break or *discontinuity* with her prior identity as a woman aspiring to marriage and family life.

When I was a young woman, I was working as a nurse. One day I met some nuns who were beautiful in spirit and had a great impact on all the doctors and patients. They seemed very joyous, loving, and at home with themselves. I began to realize that I didn't want what I had been taught to want, which was to get married and have children. I wanted to be like those nuns, to be one of them. I felt the call to join their religious order. I experienced a lot of conflict about this decision, as I had been dating a man I liked. And my mother and friends were definitely against the idea. But soon I decided to give the religious order a try, after receiving guidance and encouragement from the spiritual director of the order. He told me that my choice wasn't binding, but that I should try it out for a while. If it wasn't right, I could always change my mind and take a different direction. But if I didn't try it now I might never have that chance again. I felt that God was presenting me with the possibility of a very different direction for my life, but only I could choose whether to move forward.

Entering the order involved a series of steps that were in effect an initiation. I entered a very different culture of theological and spiritual education. I moved forward with this path, even though I had many difficult times ahead of me, full of much questioning and doubts about my religious vocation. In fact, I have experienced a constant inner crisis and struggle with my vocation that never seems to end. But these days I feel solid and at peace with my commitment, that there's nothing else that I want. I have more freedom than anyone I know. I have no personal or material shackles. Religious life has been liberating for me rather than binding or constricting.

Another example of a sudden, traumatic, and unexpected transformation of identity is seen in the case of Jane, fifty-one years-of-age, a psychotherapist and spiritual counselor, and mother of five children.

When I was thirty-seven I had a major car accident, went into the emergency room, and lost consciousness on the operating table. I went out of my body and could see everyone struggling to revive me. I felt a complete cessation of physical and emotional pain and a state of peace, and a realization of how much pain I had always been in. After that, my life began to change. I'd been addicted to drugs and alcohol and had been on medication for depression, and now all that began to change. I went back to school, even though my husband threatened to leave me if I did.

One of my first teachers was a beautiful woman with long gray hair. She taught me to meditate, and one day while I was practicing a light appeared. Then my grandmother, who had died five years earlier, was sitting next to me. I could hear her, smell her, and feel her, although I could not see her. She told me she would always be with me, and she answered some of my questions. Then she took me back into the light that I had experienced on the operating table when I had almost died. I entered a space of pure love in which I experienced being perfect and there was nothing I had to do, I was just perfect. I didn't have to be or do anything more.

Soon thereafter, sitting in a psychology class I spontaneously had the realization—not from my head but from the center of me—that I was here to work with people as a counselor. It was like being hit by a bolt of lightning, It was a peak experience— my whole body was resonating with this realization. After this, I left my husband. My teacher supported me and talked to me for hours while I fell apart emotionally. Later, I reentered the space of the light in meditation and realized I couldn't just be a traditional therapist, that I had to incorporate religion in some way and that my work was also to be a form of ministry. I realized that if I didn't do my work as a counselor I would feel unfulfilled when I die.

Jane's dramatic near-death experience and subsequent spiritual awakening led to major changes in her lifestyle. She stopped drinking and taking drugs, began to meditate, and pursued a new career.

Illumination of vocation can be associated with either heightened continuity or transformation of an established definition of personal identity. In the illumination of one's vocation some elements of identity are preserved yet one is often fundamentally changed. Other people may hardly recognize you.

Ultimately, illumination can occur anywhere, anytime. No special circumstances are necessary. What matters is a willingness to recognize your illumination when it occurs, to not ignore it or deny it, even if your intuition or interest seems to be guiding you in a strange direction.

To create a calling is to create your own myth. You have to invent yourself. You may be the postal worker who is also a dazzling photographer, or a rock climber, or a singer in a rock band, or a compassionate servant who feeds homeless people. Years ago my eye doctor had a secretary named Ethel Shine. I'll never forget how the first time I arrived to have my eyes examined she called me inside the office and spontaneously began to do a psychic reading for me. It was very accurate and very helpful. She did this for most of the patients! This was her real work in life, but she did it for free, under the cover of being a secretary in an optometrist's office. Ethel passed on several years ago, but her memory lives on in the hearts of many people whom she assisted. She had a valuable gift to share, and she fulfilled her calling quietly, without any desire to be known and recognized by the world.

Meditation on Defining Your Vocation

Sit comfortably in a chair and take several deep breaths until you are relaxed. Then take a couple of minutes to write your own myth, the myth of who you are, who you would like to become, or how you would like to reinvent yourself. Don't think about what someone else would want you to write. No one else will see this but you. In defining your personal myth, be bold and let your imagination roam freely. Don't be constrained at this stage by the bounds of what is practical or seems attainable. Think about what you would like to accomplish and who you would like to become. Record your thoughts in your journal. Contemplate these images and stories of your life's calling and add to them whenever you wish.

10

Confirmation

After illumination of our purpose or calling, it is essential that we receive some form of confirmation that this is indeed the right path for us to pursue. There are three main forms of confirmation: internal, interpersonal, and situational.

Internal Confirmation

Internal confirmation occurs through an internal sense of the rightness of a certain course of action, through a quiet knowing, or a sense that the vocation fits us. Jan, for example, stated that her work as an artist seemed natural, like it fit her personality perfectly. From the first time she attended a painting class, she had no doubt that this activity felt right to her. Internal confirmation also occurs frequently through listening to the inner voice. Something in us seems to know what is right for us, and sometimes it speaks quite directly.

Internal confirmation may also arise through the guidance of dreams. For example, after I had wandered around for over a year, I found a job as a ghostwriter that enabled me to save more money. When that job was finished, I became quite absorbed in my personal studies. All I wanted to do was to stay home and read books on psychology and spiritual growth and do my own writing and meditation. I had enough money saved that I didn't need to work for a few months. However, at one point I took a job because I thought I ought to. But what I really wanted was to be at home, because that was where I felt my most important work was unfolding. Then I had the following dream: I left the place where I had taken the job, and I walked on a little cobblestone path to a little cabin. And inside the cabin were all of my papers and books strewn everywhere. I went inside and looked through the papers, and found a perfectly symmetrical, smooth oval stone, half white and half black.

As soon as I woke up from this dream, I understood its meaning: the smooth stone, half black and half white, was a symbol of completion, integration, and wholeness. Jung would call this a symbol of the emergence of the Self, the goal of individuation. It often appears in the form of a jewel, a sacred object, a mandala, a sacred personage, a spiritual teacher, or a wise old man or woman. In my case it took the form of this beautiful stone, representing the wholeness of my essential identity. It was there waiting for me in my own place, amidst my own work. I quit my job the next day so I could go back to my real work. The dream confirmed that this was where I would find the precious object, myself.

Interpersonal Confirmation

The calling to a particular activity can also be confirmed through interpersonal confirmation. Here, one's sense of vocation is strengthened by another person, someone who acknowledges one's gifts or the fittingness of the vocation, and encourages one to pursue it further. A teacher's influence and the guidance of parents, friends, psychics or spiritual directors are commonly mentioned forms of interpersonal confirmation. We may be very shy about our interest or activity, perhaps even insisting that we're just a beginner and are not any good. But someone else may come along and tell us, "You really are very good at this. You've got a talent. You should keep pursuing this interest." This is interpersonal confirmation.

For example, when Ralph was a child other people confirmed his psychic and healing abilities and encouraged him to develop them. And describing a later period of his life, Ralph said,

> When I was 21, I met a woman who recognized my psychic abilities and helped me develop them further. I began to have the ability to heal people with my hands and tell them what was wrong with them and what kinds of treatments they needed.

Situational Confirmation

In other cases, we may receive situational confirmation of our vocation. Here, events seem to work out in such a way to confirm that a given path is the right road for us, and to enable us to pursue our vocation. A man named Paul described how an opportunity opened up for him to attend Quaker seminary, even though he had no money. "I considered attending seminary and my calling to go there was confirmed by how circumstances synchronistically worked out to allow me to find a job, a place to live, and to be able to pay my tuition."

When we are embarking upon the right path, things work out in such a way to reassure us that we are heading in the right direction. This kind of circumstantial confirmation is often accompanied by the experience of synchronicity, the meaningful coincidence of an outer event and inner attitude, decision, or realization. For example, we just happen to meet someone who teaches us something or introduces us to a new interest or activity. Or a job just happens to open up in exactly the field and geographic location we are interested in. In the first chapter of this book, I described how I unexpectedly decided to move to California to study yoga. Soon after I made this decision, I had the thought, "I should write to the *Yoga Journal* to see if there might be a job for me there." I wrote to *Yoga Journal* and the publisher, Michael Gliksohn, wrote back to me that his wife was going to be going on maternity leave at the exact time I would be coming to California, and they would be needing someone to fill in for her. He offered me a job without even having met me! I felt my decision had been confirmed.

Synchronicities appear to be coincidences, but they seem too uncanny to be due to sheer chance or accident. We've all had experiences like this: You get stuck in a line somewhere and grumble to yourself about how you hate to get delayed. Then you walk out the door and turn the corner and right there is someone you haven't seen in twelve years. If you had been there a minute earlier or a minute later, you would not have seen each other. Synchronicities reveal that we live in a meaningful universe, a coherent, intelligent field, a world that has an intention for us. If we pay attention to synchronicities, our lives are full of signposts along the way.

Our work in the calling may often feel like walking at the edge of a precipice. The important thing is to keep walking without looking over the edge to the chasm below. On the path of vocation our intention is constantly tested. Do we have the courage and faith to proceed despite the uncertainties and lack of security that this path may pose for us? Sometimes we have to go out on a limb and learn to live, as spiritual teacher Barry Tellman once said, "with both feet planted firmly off the cliff."

I believe there is a little gnome, a trickster spirit that begins to be present in our lives, who teaches us that our efforts to do our true life's work are supported. Through repeated situational confirmations, we begin to trust that we are being sustained and assisted in our efforts by mysterious hidden forces—whether we call these angels, spirit guides, the Ascended Masters, God, or the Great Spirit. These invisible forces are very patient and bestow blessings, especially at times of great suffering and hardship, when we think things couldn't possibly get worse. Suddenly there is a descent of grace, as if something is reassuring us that all is well. Somehow the rent money comes together at the last moment. Somehow the money to attend the conference, or print the magazine, or open the new store appears out of nowhere. If you're on the right path, things work out. You don't understand how it happens, but it just does.

11

Development of the Vocation

After illumination of a compelling life project or calling, we must usually undergo a period of developing the vocation by improving our skills or refining our state of consciousness to be able to better carry out the vocational task. Some common themes pertaining to the stage of development include overcoming one's own resistance to taking up a particular path; resolving emotional blocks; skill development and cultivating our natural talents or gifts; and understanding the importance of timing—the awareness that we are likely to pass through dormancy periods as well as periods of vocational fruition.

Skill Development

Most people develop their skills in a specific work by attending school, getting specialized job training, or landing a job in their field of interest. For others, skill development occurs in the context of apprenticeship, by learning directly from someone who has already mastered a particular trade, craft, or body of knowledge. A teacher or mentor may not only serve as an inspiring example to emulate, but may also support and sustain our efforts to gain confidence and skill in that work. When I was a young, aspiring musician, I took guitar lessons from several teachers. I was so excited to be able to learn from them that I lived from lesson to lesson. Each of my music teachers had a major influence on my life and became a part of my own identity.[101] Once you have experienced illumination and confirmation of your calling, throw yourself whole-heartedly into developing and deepening your skills. Learn from anyone who can teach you anything about your interest. Don't worry about when you'll be an expert. With time and experience you will develop excellence in this work.

Affirming the Vocation

An important aspect of development is the need to affirm and reaffirm the vocation, to choose it for ourselves and to periodically renew our commitment to it. Donna, who entered an order of nuns as a young woman, reported that she reaffirmed her commitment to her spiritual calling after a dream helped her resolve her feelings about a personal relationship.

Years after entering the order, there was a period when I got involved with a man. Eventually I broke up with him, and then spent years trying to forget about him. I was in so much emotional pain from this that I couldn't study or relate to people properly. I was a mess. I asked my unconscious for a dream to help me resolve this issue. That night I had a dream that brought about a profound emotional catharsis for me. I dreamt that I was standing on the Golden Gate Bridge with a friend. Somewhere below us I could see the man I was involved with leaving a restaurant. I realized I did not want to see him anymore. Quite unexpectedly my friend said, "Donna! You've got a terrible wound on your thigh!" I looked down and saw that I was indeed wounded, that my leg was covered with a large sore covered with pus. Suddenly I began to vomit and vomit, over the side of the bridge. When I was finished, my friend said, "Donna, you are healed!" I looked down and saw that the wound had disappeared. Then I woke up.

After that dream, my suffering over that relationship ended, and my peace and energy and enthusiasm for life were restored. Then I felt free inside myself again to do daily good works and to be present for others. Since that time, I have never again had a dilemma about whether I want to be married. I feel I am where I want to be.

Another story illustrating the reaffirming of a vocation was recounted to me by a minister named Jim:

I have had many conflicts with my calling over the years, and my own work is to help others, especially clergy, grapple with their calling. Some years ago I came to affirm and accept my vocation as a minister through a very unusual experience: I was watching an ant struggle to escape from a puddle of water. Suddenly the ant stopped struggling and began to swim through the puddle instead. I saw that this ant's struggle was like my struggle with my ministry and that if I wanted to, I could stop struggling and choose my vocation. In that moment, I accepted the course my life was on and chose it, instead of feeling victimized or resentful toward the Church as I had for many years. There was so much meaning in that moment. To me, affirming my vocation is also an affirmation of the intelligence of life, which guides us, leads us, and has an intention for us. I realized that I didn't need to change the form or kind of work I do, only my attitude toward it.

Adjusting the Form

In contrast to Jim's final statement, in many instances it is indeed necessary to change the form chosen to express one's personal calling in order to develop it fully. Vocation often changes over time, and it may be necessary to adjust the form of your calling or your conception of it. Finding a calling is developmental, involving not so much a one-time event as a process of embellishing and refining the form, and evolving into new dimensions of the work. The essential personal qualities that you are trying to express may remain relatively constant. It might be a nurturing presence, love, and emotional warmth and concern; or it might be psychological insight and the ability to guide others. It might be a witty mind and good writing skills, analytical abilities, or an ability to create beauty through sound or color. Nevertheless, the form chosen to express those qualities very likely will change over the course of time.

During one period of my wanderings I resided in Boulder, Colorado, where I spent some time as a street musician playing on the Pearl Street Mall. As I mentioned earlier, I harbored fantasies of becoming a professional musician. However, my efforts to start a career in music didn't fare very well. I soon learned that the music business is more competitive than I had expected and I made little headway in joining a band or getting jobs as a musician. In truth, I was a complete flop. I could play beautifully in private or for friends, but as soon as I got on stage to play in a club I was terrible! Even though I was a good musician, I was not a good entertainer. The role of professional musician didn't fit my personality. I am a somber, serious, studious person, not equipped with the kind of bright, sunny personality that can entertain a bunch of strangers in a smoky bar. My music is searching and thoughtful, but not particularly light or fun. Thus, my performances did not go over well in nightclubs. For several months I continued performing on the streets. But although this was enjoyable, I gradually began to recognize that I wasn't going to make it as a musician. It became apparent that this road was a dead-end for me. I simply wasn't going to be successful following this path.

The fact that my efforts to be a musician did not succeed illustrates that to find our life's calling we sometimes have to experiment with different roles and activities, even if might appear that we are following the wrong path for a while. Although things didn't work out for me as a professional musician, the time I spent involved in song writing and playing guitar was invaluable, enabling me to undergo an important process of self-constitution. By writing and playing songs about my quest, my dreams, my insights, and my confusion, I invented myself and my own mythos.

During this period I saw myself as something of a poet as well as a musician, and actively tried to get my work published. Unfortunately, my efforts yielded nothing but a pile of rejection notices from various publications to which I sent my writings. Nevertheless I still felt my poems were of some value. I believed in my calling to be a writer; I just hadn't found the right form.

One day the famous poet Allen Ginsberg came walking down the street and saw me with my guitar. He asked me if I could play a blues in the key of C. I hit it, and he launched into a series of loud, scandalous songs that appeared to shock a group of tourists who passed by us on the streets. Here was the embodiment of the bard, in the flesh! He was hilarious, outrageous, completely uninhibited. He had found his calling! On another occasion Ginsberg looked over a poem I had written about my travels in India and made some suggestions. In about twenty minutes, he taught me an essential lesson about how to write. He said, "What do you mean here? Why do you use these abstract terms? Tell me what actually happened, what you really saw and felt. Pay more attention to concrete facts and details." His excitement about the craft of poetry and writing confirmed for me that this was an inherently worthwhile activity—worth pursuing even if it didn't lead immediately to a job or a career. What mattered most was that it was fun! Rewriting this poem after my conversation with Allen Ginsberg helped me produce a personally meaningful statement, both comical and serious, about my ongoing quest to reconcile yogic, contemplative pursuits with a life in the real world. Here's the final version.

Embracing the Wheel

Stepping over bodies lying on the platform
wondering who's dead, who's dying,
and who is just asleep
I climb aboard the midnight train to Bombay
with hot wind blowing in my eyes
squashed together in the aisles
among young Hindu hipsters with fat wristwatches
synthetic Hawaiian design sport shirts
flashing reflector sunglasses, big grins, and shag haircuts,
fourteen-year-old mothers wearing saris
chattering or nodding off in doze,
sad-eyed working men in soiled white dhotis
exhausted from twelve factory hours
returning to their families
in windowless brown clay sunset evening homes
with a thousand unheard dreams singing in their souls
and their skinny, serious sons holding school books
with the treasured wisdom of physics, math
whatever builds machines,
while I travel from Khajuraho temples to Benares to Ajanta caves
carrying yogic scriptures in my backpack
and a mind full of mystical ideas about karma
which shield me from bewilderment.
I'm on my way back home now from the ashram
where I never got the hang of wearing lungis,
where kamikaze mosquitoes attacked me in the meditation cave,
where I wrote letters home to mom and dad
telling them how much I loved cleaning toilets
for the guru like a slave.
I'll never forget how once
I accidentally snorted spicy vegetable broth up my snout
causing me to have spasms on the holy ashram kitchen floor
and how the swamis all howled!

One day I rose at 2 a.m.
to sit on a mountain undistracted
folded my legs ceremoniously into lotus posture
breathing deeply
hoping that perhaps I'd reach samadhi
and nearly screamed when the sounds of Pink Floyd
drifted up from the Japanese tape decks
of villagers milking their cows
in the valley below.

A wise looking old gent with a tweed jacket
surveys this crowded train
and looks sadly out the window at the solemn mountains
the encampments where thousands live
under roofs of cardboard and tin
with nothing but their bodies, their fever, and their dysentery.
Cheerful billboards turn our eyes to vivid, sexy pictures
from Bombay romance films.
One sign reads, "Life is a one-way journey, why rush through it?"
while the train screams through the dark night
pounding and rocking
India Express headlines exclaim, "Parliament dissolves!"
and an evangelist preaches the savior soon to come.
A blind man inches through the crowd
mournfully singing a happy song
until a tiny wrinkled woman in a faded orange sari
places two small coins in his cup
making the man's face light into a smile
as if that one small act
was all that we could know of the eternal
as we travel through unceasing rounds
of birth and death
and change.

Writing this poem helped me reinvent myself. It doesn't matter whether or not it is a "good" poem by the academic standards of the poetry establishment. It was an expression of my identity and my journey, just as this book is. I am still a writer, although I have changed the form through which I express this part of myself. Sometimes the calling develops in ways we don't perceive right away. Old interests come full circle and we learn to use our talents and skills in new ways.

No one said the path of following your life's calling would be easy. You have to search for it by many means, earn success through hard work, and skillfully change and adapt the form used to express the calling over the course of your life. The vocation is a construction, one that requires that we bring forth various parts of our identities over time. We might think we've followed a wrong path for a while, but the wrong path helps us recalibrate our personal compasses so ultimately we can find our true path, the path that truly suits us.

Professionalizing

An important dimension of development is grappling with the question of how to ground or even professionalize our vocation. This is not required by any means, but each of us needs to make a choice: Do I need to try to professionalize this talent, interest, or pursuit? Can I earn my livelihood through this activity? Or should it remain something I pursue in addition to whatever I do to earn a living?

It is important to be practical. There are many pursuits in life that may be our central passion but that won't enable us to support ourselves economically. We may decide that it's okay if our job and our true calling are not the same thing. Wallace Stevens, one of the greatest twentieth century American poets, worked for most of his adult life for an insurance company in Hartford, Connecticut. Poetry was his central life's work, but it was not what he did for his livelihood. It wasn't practical. He had to earn a living so that he was free to pursue his life's work. And just because he didn't earn his money by writing poetry doesn't mean that he didn't achieve excellence and find fulfillment in his vocation.

In an ideal world we'd all be doing our life's calling to earn our living, but this is not always realistic. In some cases it is better to make the best of the relative stability that an established job or career gives us and then find something else we're passionate about, that's intrinsically satisfying to do, and pursue it on the side. As a culture, we tend to put all of our emphasis on money, profession, and status. However, as I've said earlier, a vocation is not always the same thing as a profession. At times it's better to delay or forego professionalizing our vocation while we continue to develop our skill and our joy in that activity. We may have to turn corners in our lives and fulfill commitments before we have the freedom and the inner and outer quietude that enables us to pursue our vocation more actively.

Be practical. You have to support yourself while you pursue your calling. Recognize that you may not be able to earn your livelihood from this pursuit immediately. It may take a while. Nevertheless, there are also moments to say, "I want to ground this work in the world. It's time for me to do this all the time and be visible and make this my primary source of livelihood." A crucial stage in development is reached when you recognize that this work is what you really want to pursue, and you become more fully committed to this path. Despite the problems sometimes involved in grounding and professionalizing a calling, many people do feel that they must make a particular activity their means of livelihood, not just an avocation.

An important question related to professionalizing is whether we need to get certification, credentialing, or some other form of recognition of our authority to practice a particular craft, skill, or profession. There are some careers that require credentials, such as a license to practice medicine, psychology, or cosmetology, or specialized training to be a criminologist, dental hygienist, or car mechanic. Other callings, however, may take one far outside the world of formal academic education, job training situations, and socially conventional careers. Many artists, creative writers, musicians, and mystics, for example, have to stand on their own in a world that often doesn't comprehend or support their works and their vision. Such individuals need to learn to affirm their own right and ability to follow this path through what psychologist Otto Rank called "the act of self-appointment." This term refers to an internal act of self-empowerment in which we stop waiting for confirmation from the world of what we want to do and just start doing it as best we can, feeling entitled to pursue it without guilt or the fear that someone else will disapprove.

The act of self-appointment is also important because it helps us pursue our paths without being scared off by the competition. The world is a competitive place, with many people trying to achieve success and prosperity through their respective enterprises. I know many people who have been scared off by all the people vying for advancement and recognition in their fields and who have given up their vocational pursuits as a result. It's important to constantly remind ourselves that we have a right to do our work, too, even if there are others working in the same field or area. If we cultivate excellence and distinction in whatever we do, and continue doing it because we love it, other people will recognize our work and support us in the ways we need.

A story that illustrates many facets of developing a true and unique calling in the world, including the process of professionalizing the vocation, was recounted to me by Bob, a forty-three-year-old man.

As a child I was told I was supposed to become something important. I tried different career paths but none of them felt right. I went into the Peace Corps and searched for an answer to the question, "What is discipline?" One day during meditation I received an inner message, "Discipline is conscientiously following your interests." I came to realize that it didn't matter what I did; it only mattered how I did it. So the worrisome question, "Who am I going to be?" became meaningless and I accepted, "This is who I am."

For many years I continued following my interests in music and gardening and natural medicine without worrying too much about having a big career. However, when I began living with a woman I learned that I needed to translate my interest into a livelihood. This was not so easy for me. What had been play now had to become work. I realized I knew nothing about making a living and how to support another person. For a long time I resented having to work for a living. But gradually I learned to earn my livelihood by following my true interests. After I married I formed several businesses: a tree-trimming business, a musical instrument shop, and a plant nursery, all of which I run out of my home. I also helped my wife form a business of her own. I still do what I've always loved doing, working outdoors, hanging out with plants, and working with wood to make instruments, but somehow I've made a career out of all of this.

If we do choose the route of professionalizing our calling, we may be confronted at times with a feeling that the essential quality of our calling has been lost as a result. For example, a friend of mine named Sarah was exceptionally gifted as an herbalist. As the years passed, however, she got tired of scrambling to survive and decided to go back to school to become a nurse, which she felt would give her greater credibility in the world to practice her healing art. In truth, this is exactly what happened. Because she was a registered nurse her belief in the efficacy of natural, plant-based remedies was taken more seriously by others, and she began to get more private referrals. But frequently she struggled with the choice she had made, because she felt that at times there was a discrepancy between the essential quality of her vocation (her inner vocation) and the form she had chosen to express it (her external vocation)—which also involved working in hospitals where her own holisic approach to treating medical problems was often met with scorn and derision by doctors and other nurses. Ideally, our inner sense of vocation gives rise to its own inherent, appropriate form of expression. However, it is possible to feel that the outer form we have chosen does not properly match our inner sense of vocation, and in such cases further adjustment of the form of our vocation is called for.

Most people who pursue a calling in life engage in a continuous process of adaptation to make their outer work match their inner vocation more closely. Once I went through a two-year training in traditional psychoanalytic psycho-therapy. I was taught to work in the classical way of acting neutral, like a blank screen upon which clients could project their own internal conflicts. But although I tried to learn this detached clinical stance, it wasn't congruent with my own identity and preferred way of working. I felt inauthentic trying to counsel others in this manner. Ultimately I found a warmer, more personal and relaxed way of interacting with clients that is more natural to me.

Internal Development

In addition to external skill enhancement and professionalizing, pursuit of a vocation also demands of us various kinds of internal development. To fulfill our calling we may need to meditate to become a more adequate embodiment of the archetype. Or we might have to resolve emotional blocks or issues that prevent us from assuming this role, doing this work, being this kind of healer or activist or businessman. This internal work enables us to be ready to be on the stage of life in role, in the vocation.

Just because we decide to become a musician or a lawyer or a carpenter doesn't mean we can do so immediately. A lot of work is necessary to develop our knowledge and skill in the vocation, as well as to develop a state of consciousness that is consonant with and adequate to the task. As noted in Part I, a particular archetype or internal "God image" may be revealed to us, but we will have to prepare ourselves extensively so that we can embody and personalize this ideal.

Here is the story of Bill, a forty-five-year-old man who works as a counselor in an inpatient psychiatric unit for adolescents.

I experienced initiation into my calling in life through a mystical experience, a sense of indescribable knowing. In that moment I knew that my task was to become an educator, helping others to overcome limiting viewpoints and concepts. This sense of vocation ripened slowly over time. For me it took the specific shape of becoming a healer through my practice of a Tibetan Buddhist meditation exercise focused on visualizing the Healing Buddha. I felt I had a direct encounter with this figure and the Medicine Buddha became a compelling image that I felt I was molding myself into—one that emphasized learning to live free of constructs about reality and dedicating myself to helping others.

This experience confronted me with the contrast between my current psychological state and the state of clarity and enlightenment that Medicine Buddha embodies. It led me to struggle with my own social and psychological conditioning and to find a way of expressing an unconditional freedom while living in society. I realized that somehow I wanted my vision of this ideal image of "healer" to transform my present limitation and smallness and ignorance, and to find a way of translating this image into reality.

I believe that my calling is to express an energetic quality associated with healing, though not necessarily taking that form specifically. Even though I am not a doctor, I view my work as a form of spiritual medicine. I attempt to inject a healing, spiritual quality into my work with adolescents. For me, vocation does not refer to the specific job you have, it's how you perform the job. My personal vocation is to be an expression of the Medicine Buddha. It is to strive toward the image of spiritual freedom that has been revealed to me, and to embody that in my life. At times, transforming and translating the image into reality has been a struggle. I make a conscious effort to not be inflated or grandiose, but rather to genuinely express an enlightened quality in the world. I believe that at times I am succeeding in doing this.

Bill's sense of identification with the Medicine Buddha led him to realize that he had to engage in an ongoing meditation practice to become the embodiment of this archetype. Similarly, an actor or actress has to engage in years of intensive training to become an instrument of dramatic performance. The image of the calling is a goal, an ideal into which we try to shape ourselves. It is not something we become instantaneously. Perceiving and defining a calling is the beginning of a path, not the end. The calling is a light ahead of us on the road, a beacon on the horizon that we walk toward. It's important that we not become too frustrated if we don't embody it immediately.

Timing

This brings us to the question of timing in the development of a vocation. There are four basic timing themes I would like to discuss. First, there are often *delays*. We want to follow a particular path but circumstances don't allow it. Maybe you want to be an artist or a poet or a healer, but you have no time or your money situation is too turbulent to allow you to relax into this work, to take classes, and to work on your craft. It's important to recognize that we might not instantly move into the completion of our vocation, that it's going to develop and evolve. This brings us back to the issue of trust mentioned earlier. Just as we have to trust that a vision of our calling will be revealed to us as a formative image around which we can organize our lives, so, too, we have to trust that we'll be shown the way to develop it and live it, to enact the calling.

On the other side of delays is the principle of *seizing the moment*. At times we get opportunities that we have to grab. For example, Donna said about her choice to join the order of nuns, "If I didn't try it now I might never have that chance again."

During the course of my wanderings I passed through a city to visit a friend briefly and happened to meet a remarkable spiritual teacher from Venezuela named Andres Takra, who had a library full of rare books on mysticism and world religions, needed an assistant, *and* could afford to pay me! I became his apprentice, which enabled me to spend hours in his library and have private lessons with him in which I learned some of the skills of spiritual counseling. I had a hard time explaining what I was doing to my parents, who were somewhat upset to learn I was getting paid by a Venezuelan shaman-mystic to sit in his house reading metaphysical books! But if I had turned down that apprenticeship saying, 'No, I've got to get a real job,' if I hadn't seized that opportunity, I might have missed the path of my destiny.

Many people feel remorse because they had a chance to pursue an interest that they let pass by. Just as we need to have the patience and wisdom to know there will be delays and that things take time, so, too, we need the boldness to seize the moment, to go for it, to go to Mexico to study with the shaman, to take the special training course, to try a different kind of a job.

The final two aspects of timing that I would like to discuss are what psychologist Larry Cochran calls positioning and positing. According to Cochran, positioning is the stage of striving to get into position and searching for the proper situation for enactment of one's calling. In contrast, positing is the enactment of position, "to posit something in the world and to actualize the spirit or tenor of one's being." [102] Positioning is a process of gradually bringing alive in one's life and actions a "symbolic role" or "central metaphor." [103] In the stage of positing, one fully enacts "a root metaphor for selfhood such as educator, apostle, artist, champion, warrior, investigator. . . . With the adoption of this state and way of being, one consolidates a vision of what to do in life." [104]

To put this in somewhat simpler terms, there is an extended period during which you work to develop your skills in the vocation. You say you want to be a writer or a photographer or a stand-up comedian. You practice, letting people know you're new at this, not fully sure of yourself. Nevertheless, you practice the role, try it on, and get comfortable with it. In this stage you also jockey for position. To succeed in any field, you need to position yourself so that when the right moment comes you will have an opportunity to demonstrate your prowess— so that others can observe your talent, and possibly offer encouragement, praise, or opportunities to advance your work.

Later, you come into public view with your work, feel in command of your faculties in that role, and become increasingly comfortable with what you're trying to do. During this stage, you build a name, a reputation in your field, or a professional practice so you can enact this central role. Enacting one's vocation is thus a process, not an event. You get a glimmer of the possibilities, develop the work, and slowly build greater confidence. Gradually you begin to express your identity through your vocation, manifesting it in the world and being seen in that role publicly.

During the stage of positioning we need to learn the wisdom of the mouse. The mouse is a humble creature that rarely calls attention to itself. Thus, there are times to remain small, releasing the desire for fame and adulation. Later, when the time comes, you will be ready to step into the spotlight, to claim your place in the great cast of humanity, your part in the cosmic play. You will stand on the mountaintop of triumph, singing your song of joy for all to hear. When that moment arrives, be thankful for all that you have, grateful to those who have helped you, and proud of all the courage and strength it took for you to follow the path to its end. Enjoy your moment, perform your role well, and celebrate other people's performance of their life's calling, too. And remember, the real validation of your work comes not from others, but from your own enjoyment of what you do.

Concrete Steps

Earlier, you wrote a description of your personal myth of your life's calling. Now, make a list of concrete steps that you can take to begin to make this myth or image of yourself become a reality. Maybe it means taking a class, or learning a new skill like accounting or business management, or taking some photos with that camera that's been sitting in your closet, or writing an article for your local newspaper. Write down things you can begin to do now, as well as things you can foresee doing in six months or a year from now. Visualize yourself taking each of these steps.

After you've written your list of next steps, it's up to you to follow through with them. If you take these steps, you'll move toward the enactment of your calling. You'll reinvent yourself and move toward your goal if you act to make it a reality, taking one small step at a time. Action is powerful. If you want to grow wealthier, or achieve enlightenment, or be a famous actor, or start your own business you need to organize yourself around this goal and dedicate yourself to making it happen. Energy follows thought. But infinitely more energy follows action. You are what you do.

12

Finding a Shared Calling: Interpersonal Dimensions

As we develop our vocation it is natural for us to want to share it with others, to receive validation and appreciation for what we are doing and to get other people excited about it. However, we should also be prepared to encounter various interpersonal struggles and difficulties. A sense of vocation is discovered in a social and interpersonal context and can never be wholly separated from the web of relationships, which will in all likelihood impact, or be impacted (either for better or for worse), by the pursuit of a vocation. As noted earlier, interpersonal confirmation can be an important source of inner certainty and confidence about vocation. Another person may confirm that a particular path seems right for you, that you are indeed talented or skilled, and that you should keep pursuing this interest or activity. However, it is also common to feel stigmatized, socially marginal, or isolated from others as a result of a vocation. In many instances, pursuing a calling requires acting in ways that defy other people's expectations or wishes.

One of the people who has taught me the most about the interpersonal dimensions of vocation is a thirty-four-year-old man named Paul. As you read his account, take note of the themes of interpersonal confirmation as well as his description of some extremely uncomfortable interpersonal dynamics that emerged as a consequence of his vocation.

I have a calling as a Quaker minister, which traditionally meant being a person who speaks regularly in meeting for worship in a way that other people acknowledge as helpful to their own spiritual lives. Quakers do not ordain ministers, but they do recognize as a minister someone who practices the discipline of emptying himself or herself so that God can speak through him. Although Quakers believe that in a sense everyone is a minister, some people like myself have a special calling to the ministry that leads to their being recognized as such by their congregation through what is called the recording of ministers. Quaker ministry is a group spiritual discipline, not an individual one like yoga, and it involves an interplay between the individual speaking to the group as a leader and spiritual guide and being led and guided by the community. It is a practice of trying to discern what God intends for you individually and for the group.

I was inspired by a book I read about Quakers and decided to attend a meeting. I felt the presence of God in the silence of that meeting and had a strong sense of homecoming. Several people later confirmed this feeling, saying that it seemed as if I really belonged there and that they strongly sensed that I was coming home. I was quickly accepted as a member of the congregation. Joining a Quaker meeting is not just an individual decision and has to be approved by a "clearness committee" that assesses the clearness of one's calling to membership.

The first time I spoke in meeting was a very scary experience. A number of people told me that they had found my words very helpful. Soon I was being encouraged by others to pursue my ministry through further study. However, my sense of my own calling has also caused me trouble. In my meeting, there were several people who believed that because Quakers do not have ordained pastors that this means Quakers do not have ministers either. This is very different from saying that everyone is a minister. As a result of this view, they began to strongly disapprove of my manner of standing up in meeting and speaking as a minister. Their disapproval of me grew to the point that people began to walk out of meeting whenever I spoke. When I confronted them about this, they told me I needed to shut up and not say anything in meeting. I struggled with this deeply, trying to discern whether God was trying to speak to me through the voice of the community, or whether they were mistaken. I concluded that they were mistaken. Finally they tried to question the appropriateness of my membership, which really made me angry. If I had not been planning to move away at that point, I would have fought this battle to the end. As it turned out, I left the congregation.

When members of Paul's congregation called into question his ministry, he experienced interpersonal conflict and the tension of trying to weigh his own conscience and sense of calling against the views of others. His inner voice told him to speak, but other people in his community gave him disconfirming feedback about his calling, suggesting that he was dominating meetings and demanding too much attention. Another important interpersonal theme in Paul's account is his description of his vocation as participating in a group spiritual discipline rather than simply an individual pursuit. Paul expressed another interpersonal aspect of the calling when he said later on,

I had always felt a calling to be married. This caused problems in some relationships where there was a calling to be in relationship but not a mutual calling to be married. However, when I met my wife, we both immediately felt the calling to be married.

A calling can emerge between any two people. This could mean two business partners with a mutual goal of profit. Or two lovers can join their minds and hearts in a shared commitment to parenting, to creating a beautiful home, to pursuing joint art or study projects, or to practicing a spiritual discipline together. The shared calling may also be to celebrate and refine the relationship itself.

A frequently mentioned interpersonal dimension of a calling is the desire to help others. The motivation to serve can at times be taken to extremes in the form of a desire to save others. In other cases, the desire to help or support others can be an explicit part of how we define our vocation. Bob, the tree trimmer, gardener, musician, and actor, said, "I feel that part of my vocation is supporting other people, not just myself. Being a husband is part of my vocation." This statement contains an important insight that all of us who seek a calling should consider. Bob's story reminds us of the importance of establishing a service orientation to life, of shifting our commitment to assisting others. Our personal vocation often brings us to the portal of the test of service, which confronts us with questions about what goals other than profit and power are motivating our actions. For more on this important topic, read Ram Dass and Paul Gorman's wonderful book, *How Can I Help?* [105]

In some instances, the emotional or financial support of others may enable us to pursue our vocation. However, very often, to follow our chosen path we must go against the wishes of a parent, a spouse, or a boss. Not everyone will share our enthusiasm. Jane's marriage ended as a result of her new calling. After her near-death encounter and her vision of white light, she told her husband she wanted to go back to school to explore spiritual growth and psychology. Her husband said that if she did this he would divorce her. She went back to school, and they got a divorce.

At times pursuing our calling leads to a loss of respect or a loss of closeness with another person. There is sometimes a price to pay for pursuing a particular call or path. You have to decide whether or not to move forward on your path even if means suffering the loss of closeness with some person or persons. This is one of the primary tensions implicit in pursuing a calling. Other people may try to thwart you or prevent you from moving ahead. They may ridicule you, withdraw their love, or make you doubt your path with a disapproving, nonsupportive attitude. Pursuit of a calling often confronts one with basic questions about whether one is trying to please others or please oneself. Moreover, finding a way to please oneself and follow one's own desires while also serving other people lies at the heart of the complexity of finding a life's calling.

Donna overcame other people's efforts to convince her not to become a nun. For her, vocation meant being present for others, but she also noted the need to be free of emotional attachment to others. As noted earlier, a personal relationship was both a challenge and obstacle to her commitment to her vocation. Her story of how the example of the nuns led her to find her own calling to a monastic life also illustrates how one may be inspired by others.

The story of how Jim, the minister, found his vocation is filled with fascinating interpersonal themes. It begins with a classic account of an illumination experience.

I received the call that led me to become a minister as a teenager, not through dramatic visions but through a quiet knowing of something Other, the Sacred, existing beyond myself. I had a feeling of deep inner peace. I told my father of my experience and he immediately took notice and took me to visit a seminary, where I was soon enrolled. Only later did I recognize that this may have been a mistake, being more a reflection of my father's interpretation of my experience than a reflection of my own vocational interest and intent. At the time, however, I was captivated by the newfound attention and respect I was receiving from others, especially my father, because of my vocational choice. For the first time in my life I had my father's attention, so I went along with seminary, even though I was following his wishes, not my own. What I really wanted was to be a psychologist! I think it's really important to distinguish the professional expression of a vocation from the inner qualities that initially define the vocation.

I feel that my vocation is to express my empathy, intuition, and caring for others, and a sense of peace, calm, and hopefulness. But while this vocation was clear, the appropriateness of the profession I picked was not clear. For a long time I experienced a conflict between my own sense of calling and the needs and expectation of the environment, and of my family. In effect, I had my vocation chosen for me, rather than choosing it myself. I think my story highlights the need to interpret your own vocational experience without letting others do this for you, possibly setting your life on a course that might not be right for you.

As we see from Jim's account, it is possible to misinterpret an illumination. When Jim reported what had happened to him, his father immediately jumped to the conclusion that his son should become a priest. And Jim went ahead with that path in order to please his father, rather than to please himself. Other people were impressed and happy with his choice. He got his father's approval and respect for the first time. For a long time Jim felt this wasn't his true calling. But as we saw earlier, Jim was eventually able to affirm his work in the ministry after years of internal struggle. But Jim's account highlights the difference between a false calling—a course in life pursued to try to please someone else—and a true calling, one to which one can assent fully and pursue even if others disapprove.

At the same time, letting someone else interpret your experience is not always a bad thing. In some Native American cultures, for example, the person who goes on the vision quest and has some kind of vision often doesn't know immediately what it means. An essential part of the quest is the return to the tribe or community where one recounts one's inner visions to an elder, who interprets one's experience and what it reveals about one's name, one's power animals or spirits, one's future, and the mission of one's life.

Vocation, Power, and Intimacy

As we saw earlier, Donald McAdams identified the power and intimacy motives as central themes of our life stories. Accounts of how people discover their callings tend to exhibit an abundance of both power and intimacy themes. While vocation may lead to an increase of intimacy with others, it can also cause a loss of intimacy that may be a direct result of the increased sense of efficacy, talent, or skill, that the discovery of vocation often entails. This loss of intimacy could be viewed as a result of envy or fear that some people may feel toward anyone exhibiting heightened personal power, creativity, or sense of mission. Or, this could be seen as an outgrowth of the inadequate linkage of a personal calling to the broader context of social needs or norms, such that the individual's actions are viewed by others as threatening or inappropriate.

As we saw in the case of Paul, the Quaker minister, sometimes pursuing a calling can result in rejection, isolation, stigmatization, or being ostracized. It's very painful to have our most deeply felt convictions and interests ridiculed, misunderstood, and trivialized by other people, who don't always understand our pursuits. We do need to thoughtfully consider the feedback other people give us and take seriously the possibility that we are interested in something that is fundamentally misguided, dangerous, or irrelevant. But that doesn't mean we should automatically be deterred by such responses. People may think you are crazy, but what is most weird today may become mainstream tomorrow. I remember when people used to ridicule me for practicing yoga. Now yoga is becoming recognized as a highly sophisticated philosophy and set of techniques for physical culture and spiritual growth that enhances the well-being of just about anybody who practices it regularly and under proper guidance. It is widely taught in corporations and health clubs and has been adopted by many athletic teams as an essential aspect of training.

Your calling may bring you closer to others with whom you share a commitment or who are walking on a similar path. In other cases, open conflict may result—whether this be with a colleague, a parent, a partner, or a child. One woman reported that her daughter said, "Mom, why are you meditating all the time? And that gross tofu stuff you make us eat makes me *sick*!"

Interpersonal crises can result from pursuing your calling. There is a stage of the spiritual path, seemingly inscribed as an initiation along the way, where you lose all your friends, where they all think you're nuts. That's the moment when it's essential to have courage and to trust your intuition, the inner voice that tells you to keep walking, with faith that you will meet new friends later on.

The Collective and Generational Sense of Calling

In some cases, the interpersonal dimension of the calling involves a sense of responsibility to others or to a collectivity, such as your family, race, tribe, or nation. This is illustrated most vividly in the account of David, a forty-two-year-old man, employed as a high school teacher.

One day about twenty years ago, while I was visiting a spiritual community in northern California, I took some LSD. Totally unexpectedly I became the agony and the ecstasy of the Jewish people, of the entire Jewish heritage. Previously, I had never been in the remotest way connected with my Jewish roots. But to my complete surprise I had this experience where I became all the passion, caring, commitment, and suffering of Jews—especially in response to historical events like the Holocaust, the pogroms, and other manifestations of anti-Semitism. It seemed to me that all of the thoughts or emotions of people connected with this heritage comprised a tangible field of energy that still exists on another plane of reality. I felt like somehow I had a responsibility to that, that here was a body that existed and that I was now responsible for continuing it—for example, by educating my children about Jewish traditions. I feel I'm not doing a very good job of this, and I feel some frustration about it. But I truly feel that I was called to be responsible to that tradition. It's a sense of responsibility to my people, to carry on my heritage.

I feel very isolated in my calling, being the only Jewish person in my community (a small town in the Pacific northwest), and I wish I had more of a support system to help me fulfill this vocation. But sometimes I also feel that in a sense this isolation is a repetition in my own life of the myth of my people and their experience of exile and suffering.

As this story illustrates so beautifully, vocation is not just a private, personal matter, but is defined within a network of social relationships, values, and roles. Although the qualities that form your vocation may be quite unique and individualized, the means available through which to embody your calling in the world is always constrained, and defined, to a considerable extent by social conditions.

A life's calling can be socially and collectively defined rather than an individualistic pursuit. In some cases the calling is to work toward societal change, to support a particular political party, a labor union, or a professional organization or guild. A shared sense of calling can be expressed through political involvement or activism, or through a shared commitment to new lifestyles. In other instances a person's sense of purpose can be shaped by a more generational sense of calling, the shared belief that those of a particular generation are called to meet certain challenges and to promote certain ideals. Each of us lives during a particular historical period, and part of our calling is to respond to, and participate in, the historical events and challenges of our era. Our individual calling often comprises a response to a social, collective, or historical situation such as war, social dislocation, or natural disaster. Think of the people who came of age during World War II, many of whose sense of calling in life was formed by the collective need to fight and defeat fascism and to protect democracy. Or think of the 1960s, when a generation of people became committed to major cultural changes and political causes like the anti-war movement. There was a shared idealism in the sixties and a sense that members of that generation were going to remake and renew the world.

Some people do not respect the basic challenges of people of other generations. "Baby-boomers" coming of age in the sixties and seventies sometimes failed to respect the struggles and achievements of their parents who grew up during the Great Depression and World War II. Today, many members of "Generation X," contending with an increasingly violent, fragmented, and technologically complex society and severe economic uncertainties, disdainfully reject the values of their ex-hippie, "Woodstock nation" parents. A sense of alienation between generations results. Each new generation has its own ideals and challenges. All of our youth and all of our elders are worthy of understanding, patience, and respect. We are each, to some extent, a product of our times. One of the measures of a true vocation is that it comprises a response to prevailing social conditions. We may create something that is essentially timeless, like a work of art, or something that is ahead of its time, like a prescient invention or scientific breakthrough. Nevertheless, in many instances a calling is also a conscious response to the historical moment, cultural situation, or social environment in which we live.

Today many people find a shared sense of calling in commitments to causes, such as preserving societal morality, fighting violence and drug use, and efforts to save the planet from ecological degradation. Other people find a shared sense of calling in involvement with church groups or religious organizations. Still others satisfy this need through the enthusiasm of mass media and sports events.

Many of us are hungry for a shared sense of calling. In 1987, an event called the Harmonic Convergence brought together thousands of people, who enacted self-created rituals of celebration to express their intention to become more attuned to the living planet, Earth. In spiritual communities a shared sense of calling can be expressed through a group commitment to a life of meditation, prayer, and communion. At the Findhorn community in Scotland, before every meal members form a circle of meditation in which they commune with the nature spirits. Here, too, we see a shared sense of purpose, a calling that is enacted with others.

The current period of history—the era of a planet overpopulated by human beings and with a rapidly diminishing base of usable natural resources—demands that we develop an unprecedented spirit of cooperation that can perhaps only be derived from recovering a common purpose, a shared sense of calling. In this context, a sense of vocation is not only an individual concern, but also a potentially crucial ingredient for planetary survival.

Too often we disregard this dimension of calling and focus solely on finding our own individual path. Think for a moment about how you can find a calling that is shared with others.

Maybe it means meeting with others to meditate, to discuss books, or to conduct group prayer or rituals. Maybe it means participating in a support group, a writer's group, a dream group, a book club, or a study group. Maybe it means linking together with others to promote a political cause such as a local initiative or political candidate. Ponder how you could work toward shared goals with other people. This is an aspect of defining and pursuing a life's calling that all of us should consider.

13

Resolving Problems and Pitfalls

Finding a life's calling can be an exhilarating path, but there are also numerous problems and conflicts that have to be dealt with along the way. As we have just seen, some of those difficulties are interpersonal in nature—such as being stigmatized, problems in relationships, being rejected by others, or being ostracized by a community. However, there are also numerous internal conflicts and pitfalls that may arise in association with a personal vocation. These may include the fear that one is not fulfilling the vocation well, a need to face difficult emotions that arise, and having to make difficult sacrifices or choices and to set new priorities, all of which may cause considerable personal suffering.

Some people like David report that they lack a support system and thus feel quite isolated. Others, like Jim, the minister, try to please other people instead of doing what they really want. His story also illustrates the potential problem of misinterpreting the calling and making a wrong choice. Donna's story illustrates the problem of having a wavering commitment to one's vocation and feeling drawn to other paths. The story of Bill, the man who aspires to become the embodiment of Medicine Buddha, illustrates the painful recognition of a discrepancy between one's ideal and one's current state or way of being. There may also be physical hazards associated with one's vocation—for example, rock climbers and law enforcement officers both face dangers in their lines of work. The case of Ralph demonstrates the potential pitfalls of devaluing the vocation or denying it altogether, or being too reliant on recognition from others. Moreover, a number of the accounts cited thus far suggest that many individuals pass through protracted periods of inner struggle over the vocation, and doubts about the guidance of their inner voice.

Pursuing a vocation isn't always a smooth, easy, or happy path. It takes much courage and hard work, and often requires moving outside conventional pathways to express your identity and uniqueness. Difficult emotions may come up, and old fears and traumas may be restimulated. In many cases this path involves going out on a precipice. You may need to go outside the circumscribed boundaries of acceptable behavior in some cases and take some very scary risks. You may also feel resentful of others for not understanding you, or feel angry at society for not supporting your efforts. I am reminded of a movie called "The Horse's Mouth," in which actor Alex Guiness plays an eccentric, brilliant artist who is dirt poor and often misunderstood by society, especially by art patrons. A young man seeks him out because he wants to become a painter, an artist, and Alex Guiness's character growls at him, "You don't want to be an artist! Don't be an artist!" We need to understand and accept that there is stigma attached to certain activities. Shamans in some cultures were greatly feared as well as greatly respected. It was recognized that they were set apart, out of the ordinary, and possessed special powers. There is a loneliness about being placed in this position, but when pursuing a vocation it often goes with the territory. To be successful in your calling requires the willingness to stand alone with dignity, overcoming feelings of self-pity and martyrdom, and finding joy in your chosen pursuits. Hopefully at some point others will rally to your cause, but there is usually a long period where you have to carry on with your work in the absence of external validation.

Of course, inner certitude about your personal mission can be taken to extremes. This brings us to another major pitfall along the path of vocation—the problem of inflation, which we discussed in Chapter 6. Ralph, the man with the childhood psychic gift, also has an illuminating tale to tell about inflation:

> I stopped doing psychic work after a few years because it felt too marginal, too much on the fringe. And I felt a stigma attached to the kind of work I was doing. One day I took some psychedelic mushrooms and had a vision of a spirit guide named Snake, who appeared in the form of a giant white cobra. His message was that I was the Messiah, that I was to save masses and masses of people, and that in order to do that I had to give up everything that I had, starting with all of my material possessions, as well as my wife and kids. After that experience I became quite split off from reality and other people. Even the family cat started to have disturbing reactions to me. At one point I gave everything away and lived out in the desert by myself for a while. I didn't understand what was bothering everybody about me. At that point I went into therapy for help. Gradually I realized I wasn't the Messiah. I had received so much attention when I was working as a psychic and healer and had actualized so much of that specialness that I had been told as a child that I would one day realize that when I lost that aura of recognition I just short-circuited. I had come to rely on all that attention from others.

It was a very shattering experience to realize that I was human, not God, and to realize that I couldn't heal myself, much less save the masses.

Since then, my journey has been to find my place in the world as a man and to make the small contribution I can make. I consider whatever individual healing I perform as just a one piece of the healing of all beings by all beings. It's a small part of the world's healing of itself. Later I decided to go back to school and study business and organizational development. This is the kind of work I am doing now, and it feels much less marginal to me, a way for me to be a healer within organizations, without specifically being known as a healer. Now I don't see myself walking through the world with people kind of around me. I see myself as one of the others, one of the birds flying in the flock together. But I always have to be watchful of my tendency to become inflated.

Ralph's story illustrates the possibility that we will become overly identified with our role, take ourselves too seriously and become grandiose or delusional. It is important that we not become identified with an archetype such as Messiah, spiritual master, or healer and lose touch with a realistic awareness of ourselves as ordinary human beings. Does a calling to a particular mission mean that we are entitled to pursue it at the expense of other people? Should we try to impose our will on others because we believe we have been called by God? This is a delicate issue because, as we saw in Chapter 6, on the path of vocation it is common to pass through a stage of inflation as one becomes captivated by a particular spiritual image or archetype.

To address this issue, the rule I like to follow is: *Enact the vocation if it injures no other.* Many tragic historical events of great magnitude (for example, the horrors of German Nazism) can be traced to the inflation of one individual who believed that he or she had a calling from God. It's possible to express a sense of calling in an insensitive or cruel manner. Thus, it is important to embark upon our calling with a sensitivity to moral issues, without stepping on anyone else's toes, and without becoming grandiose. A sense of humor and humility about one's sense of mission is essential! The commitment to not harming others is the core of what Buddhists mean by right livelihood. The flip side of this is that we mustn't become so paralyzed by fear that we will hurt someone else's feelings that we end up not acting at all. We have a right to do our work or carry out our project as long as we are not doing it to harm someone else.

In some cases pursuing a calling requires making difficult sacrifices, or choices that may have a major impact on one's life. Pat, the acupuncturist, said, "I had a spontaneous realization during a meditation exercise that my path required the sacrifice of having a normal life of family and children. My vocation has thus involved sacrifices and preparation for the role through suffering." She felt that she could not both have children and dedicate herself to her goal of becoming a healer. She had to choose between the two. It was a difficult moment for her. But the choice made itself. As she put it, "My decisions about which direction to pursue in life were really choiceless choices because I was just following my own nature." In contrast, the theme of sacrifices demanded by vocation were taken to an extreme by Ralph, who for a brief period believed that he needed to renounce his wife, children, and possessions to pursue his messianic work.

For some people, the pursuit of a calling may require some sacrifice of economic security—whether permanent or temporary. A calling is not something you do to impress other people or win their approval. It's a labor of love, a project that is intrinsically satisfying. It's something you would gladly do even if it never makes you rich or famous. There is nothing wrong with following a particular path in order to make a lot of money. But we should also recognize that our major priority in pursuing a calling might be to help others, to learn, to have fun, to disseminate ideas, to promote political change, or to dedicate ourselves to an art form.

My first guitar teacher was a quiet man in his fifties. When I would go to his small one room studio for my lessons it was obvious even to a young boy like me that he was not a wealthy man. One day he told me about his life. He had been a promising scientist and had been offered a scholarship to a graduate program that might well have launched him into quite a lucrative career. He chose instead to pursue his real love, which was music. He had toiled in complete obscurity throughout his career. There was a touch of sadness in his voice as he told me about his lost opportunity to achieve economic security. And yet when I asked him if he ever regretted his decision, he replied that he had no regrets. Then he began to play his guitar so sweetly that I was entranced. I saw that his solace and his joy came from doing the one thing he really loved, the work he was made for. While he had not found riches, he had found fulfillment in his life's calling.

In recounting this story I do not want to suggest that all of us would or should make the same choice as he did. Nor do I wish to imply that it is impossible to find financial success through one's vocation. Quite to the contrary. I would be most happy if everyone who reads this book is able to translate their true interests into a successful and financially rewarding career. It is possible to approach one's calling in a strategic and down-to-earth manner, and to take steps that make it more likely one will be successful. This might mean going to school, finding a new job in your field, preparing and following a budget, procuring a loan, or building a home business from the ground up. Success also requires a commitment to unending expansion and refinement of one's skills. Here I am simply trying to counteract the simplistic tone of many New Age and popular psychology books and to call attention to the fact that there is sometimes a tragic dimension to the path of the calling. It doesn't *always* lead to fame, wealth, and glory. Countless visionary artists, poets, composers, philosophers, and scientists, many of them far ahead of their times in their insights and ideas, have died in obscurity and penury. Finding a calling is not automatically a road to the golden palace of earthly delights. But the consolation for the sacrifices sometimes required by our vocation is the knowledge that we are doing the work that we are destined for.

I described my own struggle, and determination, to live with the consequences of my choices in a poem:

Decision

For Dane Rudhyar
"The desert calls, I follow . . . ."

April comes,
I send in my accounting to the State
pay my due to Caesar for his guns
though I hold on by a thread to keep afloat.
In the dark before the sun
I step outside the door to taste the frost
feel the earth drinking up the melting snow

watch winged ones building homes.
Waiting is over, sap stirs in the roots
though new leaves have not yet grown.
Memories of summer have haunted me
through five long months without the sun,
but while relentless freezing gales slapped my windows
I've had much time to think of my condition
of where I might travel when lakes thaw
and the children are set free.
I have entered the winter of my heart
tuned out air waves filled with static
and focused my intent upon performance
of my dharma, my truth song
wondering if I'll shipwreck
or pass smoothly through the rapids
gathering my poise, steadying my will
sailing onward, onward
into the windy open seas.

Sitting by the calm Yahara river
four huge Canadian honkers zoom in for a landing
drenching me with soft migrant splash.
I think of Al Ghazzali
who burned with desire to be consumed in higher knowledge,
who called God the great upsetter of our hearts and our positions.
Ghazzali held back from the calling
for fear his reputation would be lost
his career become a shambles
his loving wife estranged
until a visionary angel's voice resounded
"To the road! To the road! Delay not your departure!"
I have not spoken with angels
but I too have departed
severed umbilicords of fear
and cast myself out into the wild forests of unfolding
into my state of self-imposed exile in Wisconsin.

Every day I live with my decision
to choose this tundric wilderness
as the place to plant a garden
though a bottle of massage oil
has sat next to my bed for a year
collecting dust.
When the desert called I followed
now from desert I emerge
with vision bestowed on me by night.

In some instances pursuing our calling leads to a loss of credibility in the eyes of some person or group of people. Carl Jung, a longtime student of Sigmund Freud, paid a great price when he began to develop his own ideas. He lost the friendship of his mentor and became something of an outcast from his former colleagues in the psychoanalytic movement. While Jung did experience some loneliness and sense of exile as a result, he had to follow his own calling, his own path of spiritual and intellectual development. Frequently he was assailed by doubts about his work. Nevertheless, he persevered and went on to become a towering figure of modern psychology. Similarly, I know physicians, dentists, and optometrists who have begun promoting new, holistic approaches to their work that in some ways contradict the prevailing models in their professions, leading in some cases to harassment, public attack, and even loss of licensure.

Another conflict is a feeling of inadequacy or failure. One may berate oneself or lose heart. There is also the potential pitfall of being unable to find a sense of vocation. In such cases it is important to stay focused on the stage of preparation, patiently searching, no matter how long it takes.

A common problem associated with pursuing a calling is resentment over having to work at another job to make a living. We wish we could pursue our vocation more actively, but find ourselves occupied with other, more mundane, activities that demand our attention. It's important to get over the resentment of having to work. We need to have a certain toughness to carry the calling through to completion. Starving artists, mystics, and intellectuals who resent the world for not recognizing their talents often need to grow a thicker skin so they can cope with the world. Rather than compromising their artistic or intellectual talents, such people can develop a deeper maturity that greatly enhances their work.

As Ralph's story illustrated earlier, at times we may devalue the calling, deny it, or turn from it altogether. Or we may reach the point of saying, "What's the use? I'm never going to make it. It's not really that important to me. It's not what I really want." Turning from the calling is also associated with internal doubts, where our commitment wavers and we begin to wonder if we should be doing something else. Donna, for example, described how she came to question her vocation and for a time actively considered leaving the nun's order. Ultimately, however, she reaffirmed her path.

As I said earlier, we must constantly choose and reaffirm the path of our vocation, for our doubts never end. Robert Powell, a friend of mine who is an excellent guitar player, said to me a few years ago "I'm considering going back into floor tiling. I'm sick of just scraping by as a musician. I need to make some money." But that wasn't his real calling. He had paid his dues tiling floors for years. Now it was time for him to do his real work. He stuck with the guitar and is now doing fine as a professional musician, by the way. The calling can at times mean reaffirming our current pursuits, embracing them with a new passion and dedication. We often don't have to look very far at all to find our life's calling; we can simply start doing whatever we are already doing—whether it's raising a child, being a lawyer, waiting tables, or playing in a symphony—with greater reverence and contentment.

14

Building a Sacred Vessel:
Vocation as a Spiritual Path

A calling is ultimately more than a process of satisfying personal ambitions. In a deeper sense, it is a spiritual path, a way of transforming our life into a sacred vessel of Spirit. In this chapter, I will explore some of the spiritual dimensions of the calling and show how it turns us toward concerns, and a way of life, that can best be characterized as transpersonal.

For the past thirty years, a global spiritual renaissance has been occurring. More people than ever before are searching for ways of living in a spiritually conscious way, retrieving essential teachings from the world's great religions, spiritual traditions, and schools of esoteric knowledge—which have passed on techniques and doctrines to lead human beings toward enlightenment and expanded consciousness.

A new field has even emerged within the broader discipline of psychology that focuses on understanding the spiritual dimensions of human existence: transpersonal psychology. Transpersonal psychologists study nonordinary states of consciousness; religious, ecstatic, and mystical experiences; paranormal phenomena, such as telepathy, out-of-body experiences, and extraordinary physical capacities; and the effects of practices such as meditation and shamanic journeying. They investigate such topics as trance states, kundalini awakening, spiritual healing, memories associated with biological birth, past-life recall, identification with plant and animal species and with the earth itself, encounters with spirit guides, and experiences of cosmic consciousness.[106] A brief consideration of the meaning of the term *transpersonal* will help illuminate the spiritual dimensions of a calling. According to Bryan Wittine,

> The word "transpersonal" (from the Latin *trans*, meaning "beyond, through" and *persona*, meaning "mask"), was adopted to reflect the reports of individuals who were practicing various meditative techniques and experiencing states of consciousness extending beyond the customary ego boundaries and the ordinary limitations of space and time. It has also been defined as referring to the release of transcendental attributes, such as altruistic love and compassion, through the daily activities of the personality. The word can also be seen simply as an amalgam of "transcendental" and "personal." One purpose of transpersonal psychology, then, is to help us integrate the transcendental or spiritual and the personal dimensions of existence, to help us to fulfill our unique, creative individuality while pointing toward our rootedness in the deep, nontemporal, formless dimension of eternal Being.[107]

As Wittine suggests, while transpersonal psychologists focus on mystical experiences and altered states of consciousness, they are also concerned with self-transcending action, action *through* the personality, such as that often inspired by a vocation—a central life project that is felt to be impelled by a higher will, transpersonal Self, or spiritual source. Finding a calling is often a transpersonal experience in both of these ways.

The illumination of a personal calling often occurs during, or in the aftermath of, a mystical experience or altered state of consciousness in which we perceive radically new possibilities for ourselves. In such moments of heightened clarity, we gain a more vivid awareness of our total existential condition, form a new interpretation of reality, and perceive new visions of our essential place in creation. Illumination can occur when experiencing the peace and beauty of nature, in states of deep meditation, or through ecstatic dancing or drumming. Sessions of dynamic techniques such holotropic breathwork, rebirthing, and past-life regression are often mentioned as settings in which illumination occurs.[108] A vision of our vocation may arise in association with a sense of inner peace or a spontaneous inner knowing. Some people report receiving a message in a dream, or from the "higher self." As Pat stated earlier, "An inner voice guided me to my vocation. I was guided to clear up my relationship with my parents so that I would be free to leave my home town. . . ."

In addition to messages from the mysterious inner voice, we may also receive guidance through the psychic insights of others. Many people report receiving guidance about their paths from psychics, disembodied teachers and gurus, and from the spirits of deceased relatives. Awakening to one's vocation can also be connected with visions of non-physical "spirit beings," moments of religious conversion, or ecstatic experiences during meditation. In Chapter 1, I described my own experience of blissful energy and joy. David had a vision of his calling to reembrace Judaism during a psychedelic drug excursion. Jan discovered her calling as a painter in the context of purported past-life memories. She began to spontaneously receive psychic insights and developed the capacity to see other people's auras. Ralph found that he had a gift for healing other people with his hands and for perceiving their thoughts psychically. Bill had an enlightenment experience revealing a state beyond conceptual constructs and limitations. This experience became the foundation of his calling to become an embodiment of Medicine Buddha.

Jane described how her calling emerged after a near-death experience followed by an experience of pure light and a vision of her deceased grandmother, who answered many of her questions. Later, she said,

> After the experience with my grandmother, I was very open psychically and began to do psychic readings for people and soon had a thriving business. All of this happened within six months of my accident. It was a very traumatic and sudden change in my life. My own spiritual experiences were very dramatic and included kundalini experiences, visions, spontaneous chanting and bodily movements during meditation, and hearing beautiful inner sounds.

However, in addition to her report of extraordinary mystical experiences, Jane goes on to suggest how developing her vocation is enabling her to anchor her spiritual unfolding in the world. Her account leads us back to the idea of building a sacred vessel. She said,

> All of those mystical experiences have ceased for me right now while I go through a period of grounding in my life, establishing a counseling practice. I felt I could no longer contain those experiences productively until I developed more skills and more confidence in my work. So that is what I'm doing now. I have been told by my inner spiritual guides that all of these other experiences will open up again later on. I

view my work as my way of coming closer to God, and my way of paying back for all I have been given in life. It is my reason for being here on this earth. There would be no meaning in life without it.

Her account of finding a new, spiritual profession after her inner awakening illustrates how transpersonal experiences—in which our usual forms of perceiving, thinking, feeling, and self-awareness are either transcended or extended—may transform us profoundly by revealing a new sense of vocation. Mystical states of consciousness focus our awareness, at least temporarily, somewhere beyond or outside ourselves, but their end result is often to lead us back into renewed engagement in the projects of our personal lives and identities. Such transpersonal experiences often inspire creative activity, based on a sense that our life is following a pattern ordained and intended, whether by God or by our "innate potentialities."[109] As Ken Wilber has shown, our evolution into higher states of consciousness must be complemented by a growth of our capacity for *involution* —"the way we bring spirit into life and animate it, and incarnate it in a joyful and expressive way."[110]

Spiritual growth is not, in most cases, a linear ascent toward enlightenment, mystical vision, or union with God. Rather, it is a path involving a constant interplay between breakthroughs into transpersonal realms of consciousness and the growth of form of a personal vocation. Jane's story illustrates the need for a personal "container" for transpersonal experiences, a vehicle through which the new vision, energies, and insights gained in expanded states of consciousness can be grounded. Her story reminds us that breakthroughs in consciousness constantly ask to be accompanied by shifts in the nature, the quality, and the intention of our activity in the world.

While a vocation may arise in connection with a variety of extraordinary spiritual or religious openings, it also helps us stay focused on the challenges of living on planet Earth, in a body, in a particular time and place. I have observed that very often spiritual seekers, having tasted timelessness and formless realms of pure Spirit, become world weary and begin to long for retreat. Like Dave (the man we discussed in Chapter 5), our pursuit of spiritual paths and practices may still leave us confused about our direction in the world. Dave, in a classic example of what John Wellwood calls "spiritual bypassing," has attempted to transcend the challenges of building a stable personal identity prematurely.[111] The end result in such a case is not an illumined mystic but a confused person drifting without course or anchor. Dave has had many mystical, transpersonal experiences (for example, visions of light, precognitive experiences, and opening of chakras), yet none of these has enabled him to feel that his personal life has meaning or purpose. Both he and I would assent to the idea that enlightenment or spiritual growth is an important goal for his life. But to say this is not, practically speaking, sufficient, unless Dave can find a way to translate his transpersonal experiences into a vocation, a meaningful life project, a specific course of activity that integrates his inner spiritual life and his sense of purpose in daily living.

In pursuing a calling we participate in the downward movement of Spirit—in which the love and inner vision gained through spiritual attunement, contemplation, prayer, and other nonordinary states of consciousness move through us into the world. We begin to recognize that the experience of enlightenment or expanded awareness is only the beginning of a process that can eventually transform us into instruments of a creative, or even divine, force that is seeking to manifest itself fully in nature.[112] Spiritual or transpersonal growth is not just a process of "transcending the ego." It is also a process of transforming ourselves into a spiritually infused personality that can embody qualities like love, mercy, power, vision, humor, beauty, endless patience, moral acumen, and creative inspiration. Direct experiences of our connection with God, the light of consciousness, sacred presence, or pure awareness often inspire us to build a vessel in our lives in which this sacred presence, reality or consciousness can dwell. In a life dedicated to a calling, self-actualization and self-transcendence converge, and the energies of Spirit or illumined awareness begin to be expressed through us in a personally and socially meaningful way.

John, the environmentalist, experienced an ecstatic epiphany in nature in which he experienced the intelligence and consciousness of trees and a sense of oneness, beauty, and perfection. This episode, coupled with the nadir experience in the clear-cut forest, led him to recognize the inherent right of other life forms to exist; and this awareness in turn led to the realization that his vocation is not just to live for himself but to act on behalf of trees and endangered species:

These developments have shifted my own priorities and sense of calling considerably. Before I was only concerned with having a career, a reputation, and a lot of money. Now, I feel like I'm not just living for myself. I believe that Mother Earth will take care of me and all of us, but that it's my responsibility to take care of her, too. So that's how I view my calling in life now: to live in balance with nature, to try to save the Earth's natural beauty, to be an environmentalist, an activist, and a protector of the Earth. I feel proud of what I do, but I do it because it feels right, because it's the only intelligent thing to do, to try to preserve the web of life that sustains us. Having some special individual calling seems less important to me now than to be a protector of the Earth and all its wild creatures. The old life makes no sense to me any more. I keep walking on this path without knowing where it will lead or whether my efforts will be successful. Mainstream society culture doesn't seem to understand people like me. But I am grateful I have friends who share similar commitments and role models like Henry David Thoreau and John Muir. Otherwise I'd probably think I'm a little crazy.

This account illustrates how our vocation can be a more-than-individual concern, inextricably connected with social, collective, or moral concerns. A calling can be a spiritual, transpersonal path, not only because it might originate in mystical experiences, but also because of the way it releases us from self-centered preoccupations and inspires us to engage in self-transcending action—transpersonal activity.

The call may also be to pursue a spiritual path intensively. Deborah, a forty-seven-year-old dentist, gave up her job to go on a lengthy meditation retreat in India.

After my daughter went off to college, I started to feel this inner burning to pursue my spiritual practices more deeply. I had an opportunity to study with this amazing teacher with a very small, intimate group of students. I realized that this was the opportunity of a lifetime and that if I really wanted to reach enlightenment I had to go on this retreat. I knew it was a major decision. But once I made up my mind, my house sold rapidly and everything came together.

Once I was there a whole new life started for me. As soon as I arrived at the monastery I felt as if I was coming home. Meditating that much was difficult, but it transformed me profoundly. I felt as if all my life I had been fulfilling responsibilities so I could finally have this experience of inner freedom and clarity, so I could embark on this inner journey of mindful awareness. I stayed over there for three years. I continued to practice dentistry, but now I did it for poor people in a rural clinic in India, not for wealthy people in America. That experience taught me to do my work as an offering of service, a way of being helpful instead of just a way for me to earn money.

Deborah has reached a stage where committing herself to a spiritual practice is fully appropriate, not a premature attempt to transcend personal problems. She has set her feet firmly on the path to one of the highest callings a human being can embrace: the calling to awaken, to achieve true enlightenment. Note, however, that as she pursues this path, she is doing so with a firm grounding in a form of compassionate action and service, sharing her inner peace and illumination through a well-developed vocation. Like Deborah, each of us can build a sacred vessel, dedicating ourselves to the goal of spiritual awakening and making ourselves instruments of healing and light through the work of our vocation.

15

Defining the Meaning of Your Vocation

Finding a calling gives us a sense that we are unfolding according to a larger design—a realization that makes our lives feel focused and purposeful. When our vocation becomes clear, we become peaceful and inwardly certain that we are on the right path, especially if events seem to support our chosen course. This inner peace in turn supports and promotes our spiritual development, giving rise to feelings of contentment and joy. Our calling becomes the source of the meaning of our lives.

The stories we have examined illustrate some of the complex, individualized meanings vocation can have; it means something different to everyone. For Jan, it is the expression of a unique individual talent. In contrast, David's vocation focuses on the life of a collective body that exists independently of him but to which he feels responsible. He also sees a parallel between his own isolation in the calling and the history of exile and suffering of his people. Paul also noted that his vocation involves a responsibility to a group (his Quaker congregation) as well as inner responsiveness to God's intention. For Paul, vocation involves an internal attunement to the will of God, which at times enables him to express insights that others find useful. It is an inner knowing and sense of rightness that may also at times bring a person into conflict with others.

Donna stated that initiation into vocation awakened her to "something larger trying to complete itself through me." However, the demands of vocation may require acting counter to other people's wishes or expectations, and involves a protracted inner struggle with alternative paths and choices. Donna believes there is an active intelligence that guides us forward on our paths. However, it is up to the individual to follow the call that is given. Her story also teaches us that a calling constantly needs to be renewed and reaffirmed.

Ralph's vocation is to express a skill he has possessed since childhood. Circumstances and events help confirm the gift. However, internal conflict may be faced in learning to use one's talent or gift to help others. He views the individual healing he performs as a piece of "the healing of all beings by all beings. . . , the world's healing of itself." Vocation is not just an individual life project, but also means doing one's own part in collective evolution. Thus, a calling is not necessarily just an expression of an individual talent or personal mission, but can also refer to actions impelled by an attunement with a collective, spiritual, or transpersonal will seeking to unfold itself through us. For John, this transpersonal calling takes the form of action to save the physical environment from destruction.

We have seen that there are societal, individual, or transpersonal dimensions of a calling. At the societal level, vocation refers to a social role one is expected to fulfill by virtue of family, class background, or cultural tradition. Most working people in our culture do not view their work as a spiritual life-calling. In such cases, the societal level of vocation refers to work that is simply a way of earning a livelihood. However, the societal level of vocation can also refer to endeavors focused on socially defined or directed tasks and achievements that we consciously affirm as central parts of our lives.

In contrast, nearly all of the individuals whose stories we have discussed described an individual calling of some kind. Here work becomes more than just an occupation, and takes on the character of a personally meaningful task or project that fulfills one's talents, skills, and interests, and that can be expressed in the world. We have also seen a number of cases in which a transpersonal dimension of vocation was joined with its societal and individual facets, leading to a profound feeling of integration and meaning in life.

Think for a few moments about your calling. How do you define it? How does pursuit of this goal affect your attitudes and beliefs about life, evolution, your place in the universe? What are the social dimensions of your calling? How does it respond to the needs of some group or political cause? In what ways is it a perfect expression of your individuality? And what are its spiritual dimensions? How has your work been inspired by an inner vision or directive? Note how your calling integrates your life, balancing these three basic dimensions of human concern and existence—the social, the personal, and the transpersonal. When you reflect deeply on these questions you will begin to know the meaning of your calling. Knowing this, your life's purpose will also be clear.

The path to your calling may not be a direct one. It may lead through a forest of uncertainty and periods of disorientation.

You may experience a slow death of your old identity and of old values and priorities before a new self and new goals emerge. Beloved friends may not be willing to venture into the forest with you, and some may need to be left behind. It takes courage to find your calling, courage to tell others about it, and even more courage to carry it through. And efforts to find your life's calling have to be sustained. Don't expect guidance, clarity, and success to come immediately. It takes time, effort, struggle, tears, patience, faith. You have to cry for the vision, and to be willing to listen to the message or vision that comes—even if it seems totally weird! You must be willing to respond, to meet the call.

Envisioning your calling is the beginning, the root of the tree of vocation. Then a miracle happens: you shed the old skin, go beyond your fear, and start making it happen. Deconditioning is an important step: You can't move ahead with your work while the fear of parental and societal disapproval is weighing you down. You have to be courageous, a man or woman of power conjuring yourself into existence. Finding your calling is a process of creating your personal mythos and then enacting it in your life. It is often a revolutionary act, in which you break barriers and express the spirit of invention, bringing something new into existence.

When you find your life's calling, the road opens before you, and you understand that all obstacles are tests and view them as opportunities to refine your vision and your skill in executing the task. A sense of humor and a deeper faith in life's intelligence begin to be familiar companions. A profound joy begins to pervade daily life as you develop a work that expresses your uniqueness, that unparalleled configuration of spiritual, archetypal, and personal qualities and potentials that *you are*.

The funny thing is that *only you know* what is right for you. Others may think you are crazy, but it doesn't matter because *you know*. That knowing is confirmed by a variety of means: an inner voice, a psychic reading or an I Ching hexogram that speaks with stunning clarity to your situation, a seemingly chance encounter with someone that changes you profoundly. Nobody but you knows what your path should be. Maybe it means taking a job in corporate America, or going to medical school, or forming a collectively owned business. Maybe it means becoming an organic farmer in Idaho or traveling to the Yucatan. Maybe it means running for city council, or senate, or mayor. Maybe it means becoming a journalist, a solar energy expert, a homeopath, a merchant, a chef, a bohemian writer or angelic artist, an adoptive parent, or a Zen golf guru. There are thousands of roles looking for actors to perform them.

Ideally, your calling aligns you with all of creation, and with all beings. It is not about making yourself special or all-powerful or superior. It is about finding your appropriate place and utilizing some God-given talent or interest to benefit, to amuse, to liberate, or to serve others in alignment with a greater purpose—the divine plan, the relief of suffering, the evolution of our planet. You are just another tree in the forest, and yet you can emanate light—the glow of creativity and intelligence and discovery.

In the Bhagavad Gita, Krishna tells Arjuna, "Do not try to live the dharma of another." Roughly translated, this means *don't compare*. The less you compare, the more fully you can embrace your own unfolding, your uniqueness. Maybe you are primarily a seer. Maybe you are a person of action. Perhaps a union organizer, political visionary, shy musician, dedicated worker, cartoonist or satirist, outrageous poet. Simply be that fully—live to the hilt your own archetype. Stay in balance, stay on your feet, and stay in the world, unless your call is clearly outside the world toward a life of retreat and solitude.

Safe paths are fine. But less safe paths are also fine. Finding a life's calling could mean managing a grocery store, working as a bank teller, running a tractor through the fields, or doing any one of a thousand jobs with love, consciousness, and patience. Or it could mean doing something more unconventional like touring with a reggae band or becoming a multi-media performance artist. What matters is the meaning you find in your work as a means not only of self-sustainment but also of self-expression and contribution to the world and fulfillment of your personal potentials. Above all, your vocation should be an intrinsically satisfying activity—one that you love so much you can't stop thinking about it. Your calling is the axis your life revolves around.

16

Conclusion

Vocation is one of the perennial stories of humanity, a myth that draws together our social, individual, and spiritual concerns into a harmonious unity. It is a story that bestows upon our activities or goals the power of a mandate, something that is intended, purposeful, and of social, personal, or universal significance. It describes how we fulfill the needs of some greater totality and how the cosmos seeks to unfold itself through our lives, our actions.

Finding a calling is a process of preparation and meeting of prerequisites, followed by illumination of purpose in a variety of settings. Hearing the inner call, we then must follow it, despite the sometimes disruptive consequences. The initiation that leads us forward on this pathway can occur in many settings and the vision appears in many forms. The work of our vocation must be developed and trained, and various events lead to confirmation of the essential rightness of this task or project. Individual relationships are affected for better or for ill as a result of receiving a vocation, and many internal problems, pitfalls, and conflicts must be met along the way. But ultimately we can find a shared sense of calling that connects us more closely to our loved ones, our community, our society as a whole—even to the planet Earth itself. We can discern a calling through a mystical experience or it may give rise to new forms of transpersonal activity. A calling becomes a spiritual path as we learn to refine ourselves to become more adequate agents for our life tasks, more joyful, free of purely selfish motivations, more willing to serve others, and able to perceive a need in the world that is longing to be addressed and fulfilled.

Finding our vocation is one of the experiences that ultimately makes our lives fulfilling. It is the organizing theme that transforms the scattered fragments of our lives into a spiritually meaningful whole. It is a window from which we see a vision of our future. A vocation is a verse of the great song of creation, revealing our place and function in the vast universe, which is always calling to us, beckoning.

Notes

1. C. G. Jung, "The Development of Personality," *Collected Works* (Vol. 17) (Princeton, NJ: Bollingen, 1934), pp. 175–76.
2. H. Jonas, *The Gnostic Religion* (Boston: Beacon Press, 1958).
3. M. Fox, *Original Blessing* (Santa Fe, NM: Bear Books, 1985).
4. M. Eliade, *Rites and Symbols of Initiation* (New York: Harper & Row, 1958).
5. H. Chaudhuri, *Sri Aurobindo: Prophet of Life Divine* (San Francisco: Cultural Integration Fellowship, 1973), pp. 48–49.
6. R. Bellah, R. Madison, W. M. Sullivan, A. Swidler, & S. M. Tipton, *Habits of the Heart* (Berkeley: University of California Press, 1985).
7. S. Krippner (Ed.), *Dreamtime and Dreamwork* (Los Angeles: Tarcher, 1990), p. 3.
8. D. Feinstein & S. Krippner, *Personal Mythology: The Psychology of Your Evolving Self* (Los Angeles: Tarcher, 1988).
9. J. Campbell, *Historical Atlas of World Mythology* (Vol. 1) (San Francisco: Harper & Row, 1983).
10. S. Krippner, "Dreams and the Development of a Personal Mythology," *Journal of Mind and Behavior*, 7 (1986): 449–62.
11. R. Lannoy, *The Speaking Tree: A Study of Indian Culture and Society* (New York: Oxford University Press, 1971), p. 217.
12. A. T. de Nicolas, *Avatara: The Humanization of Philosophy Through the Bhagavad Gita* (New York: Nicolas Hays, 1976), p. 172
13. S. Aurobindo, *The Essential Aurobindo*, R. McDermott (Ed.) (New York: Schocken, 1973), pp. 115–17.
14. R. Shaw, *The Call of God: The Theme of Vocation in the Poetry of Donne and Spencer* (Cambridge, MA: Crowley Publications, 1981).
15. H. Goldman, *Max Weber and Thomas Mann: Calling and the Shaping of the Self* (Berkeley: University of California Press, 1988), p. 36.
16. Ibid., p. 39.
17. M. Weber, *The Protestant Ethic and the Spirit of Capitalism* (New York: Charles Scribner's Sons, 1958).
18. H. Goldman, op cit., p. 24.
19. M. Weber, *The Sociology of Religion* (Boston: Beacon, 1922/1963).
20. H. Goldman, op cit., pp. 48, 110.

21. D. Ingram, *Habermas and the Dialectic of Reason* (New Haven: Yale University Press, 1987), p. 79.

22. Ibid., p. 51.

23. E. Conze, *Buddhism: Its Essence and Development* (New York: Harper & Row, 1975).

24. K. Jones, *The Social Face of Buddhism: An Approach to Political Activism* (London: Wisdom Publications, 1989), pp. 15, 19.

25. Ibid., pp. 124–25.

26. Ibid., p. 71.

27. Ibid., p. 123.

28. Ibid., pp. 64, 160.

29. Ibid., pp. 160–71.

30. Ibid., p. 139.

31. Ibid., p. 144.

32. I bid., p. 241.

33. P. Fleischman, *The Healing Spirit: Explorations in Religion and Psychotherapy* (New York: Paragon House, 1989), pp. 62, 64.

34. Ibid., p. 63.

35. Ibid., p. 65.

36. I. Progoff, *The Dynamics of Hope* (New York: Dialogue House Library, 1986), p. 78.

37. Ibid.

38. Ibid., pp. 180, 189.

39. Ibid., p. 189.

40. R. Adams & J. Haaken, "Anti-Cultural Culture: Lifespring's Ideology and Its Roots in Humanistic Psychology," *Journal of Humanistic Psychology*, 27 (1987): 501–17.

41. Ibid., p. 505.

42. H. Kohut, *The Restoration of the Self* (New York: International Universities Press, 1977), p. 99.

43. A. Samuels, *Jung and the Post-Jungians* (New York: Routledge, 1985), pp. 105–6.

44. C. G. Jung, "The Structure and Dynamics of the Psyche," *Collected Works* (Vol. 18) (Princeton, NJ: Bollingen, 1960), p. 399.

45. E. Whitmont, "Archetypal and Personal Interaction in the Clinical Process," in N. Schwartz-Salant & M. Stein (Eds.), *Archetypal Processes in Psychotherapy* (Wilmette, IL: Chiron Publications, 1987), pp. 7, 4.

46. N. Schwartz-Salant, "Patriarchy in Transformation: Judaic, Christian, and Clinical Perspectives," in M. Stein & R. L. Moore (Eds.), *Jung's*

Challenge to Contemporary Religion (Wilmette, IL: Chiron Publications, 1987), p. 50.

47. Ibid., pp. 53–7.

48. V. Turner, *The Ritual Process* (Chicago: Aldine, 1969).

49. J. Hall, "Personal Transformation: The Inner Image of Transformation," in L. C. Mahdi, S. Foster, & M. Little (Eds.), *Betwixt and Between: Patterns of Masculine and Feminine Initiation* (La Salle, IL: Open Court, 1987), p. 333.

50. L. C. Mahdi, "Introduction," in L. C. Mahdi, S. Foster, & M. Little (Eds.), *Betwixt and Between: Patterns of Masculine and Feminine Initiation* (La Salle, IL: Open Court, 1987), p. 11.

51. M. Eliade, op cit.

52. S. Foster, & M. Little, "The Vision Quest: Passing From Childhood to Adulthood," in L. C. Mahdi, S. Foster, & M. Little (Eds.), *Betwixt and Between: Patterns of Masculine and Feminine Initiation* (La Salle, IL: Open Court, 1987).

53. M. Eliade, op cit.

54. A. Bharati, *The Ochre Robe* (Garden City, NY: Doubleday, 1970).

55. J. Halifax, *Shamanic Voices* (New York: Dutton, 1979), p. 6.

56. R. L. Moore, "Ritual Process, Initiation, and Contemporary Religion," in M. Stein & R. L. Moore (Eds.), *Jung's Challenge to Contemporary Religion* (Wilmette, IL: Chiron Publications, 1987), p. 148.

57. Ibid., p. 155.

58. V. Hine, "Self-Created Ceremonies of Passage," in L. C. Mahdi, S. Foster, & M. Little (Eds.), *Betwixt and Between: Patterns of Masculine and Feminine Initiation* (La Salle, IL: Open Court, 1987), pp. 304 ff.

59. E. Sullwold, "The Ritual Maker Within at Adolescence," in L.C. Mahdi, S. Foster, & M. Little (Eds.), *Betwixt and Between: Patterns of Masculine and Feminine Initiation* (La Salle, IL: Open Court, 1987), pp. 112–3.

60. A. Stevens, *Archetypes: A Natural History of the Self* (New York: William Morrow, 1982), p. 164.

61. A. Maguire, "Jung's First Dream," in L.C. Mahdi, S. Foster, & M. Little (Eds.), *Betwixt and Between: Patterns of Masculine and Feminine Initiation* (La Salle, IL: Open Court, 1987), p. 61.

62. C. G. Jung, "Aion: Researches Into the Phenomenology of the Self," in *Collected Works* (Vol. 9) (Princeton, NJ: Bollingen, 1959), p. 225.

63. C. G. Jung, "Concerning Mandala Symbolism," in *Collected Works* (Vol. 9) (Princeton, NJ: Bollingen, 1959).

64. D. Feinstein & S. Krippner, op cit.

65. M. W. Heery, "Inner Voice Experiences: An Exploratory Study of Thirty Cases," *Journal of Transpersonal Psychology*, 21 (1989): 74.

66. C. G. Jung, "On Synchronicity," in *Collected Works* (Vol. 8) (Princeton, NJ: Bollingen, 1951).

67. Ibid.

68. D. Rudhyar, *Rhythm of Wholeness* (Wheaton, IL: Quest, 1983).

69. D. Rudhyar, *The Astrology of Personality* (New York: Lucis Trust, 1936), and *Person Centered Astrology* (Santa Fe, NM: Aurora Press, 1976).

70. For more on this topic, see S. Arroyo, *Astrology, Karma, and Transformation* (Sebastopol, CA: CRCS Publications, 1978); G. Bogart, *Astrology and Spiritual Awakening* (Berkeley, CA: Dawn Mountain Press, 1994); and S. Forrest, *The Inner Sky* (New York: Bantam, 1984).

71. R. L. Moore, op cit.

72. M. Buber, *I and Thou* (New York: Scribners, 1970), p. 92.

73. Ibid., pp. 103, 108–9.

74. R. Assagioli, *Psychosynthesis* (New York: Penguin, 1976).

75. Ibid., p.126.

76. M. Brown, *The Unfolding Self* (Los Angeles: Psychosynthesis Press, 1983).

77. Ibid., p.142.

78. D. Rudhyar, *Rhythm of Wholeness*, op cit.

79. Ibid.

80. Ibid., pp. 224, 226.

81. D. Rudhyar, *Culture, Crisis, and Creativity* (Wheaton, IL: Quest, 1977), and *The Astrology of Transformation* (Wheaton, IL: Quest, 1980).

82. G. Bogart, *Culture, Crisis, and Creativity: The Prophetic Vision of Dane Rudhyar* (Berkeley, CA: Dawn Mountain Press, 1993).

83. Donald Rothberg, personal communication.

84. C. G. Jung, "The Relations Between the Ego and the Unconscious," in *Collected Works* (Vol. 7) (Princeton, NJ: Bollingen, 1953).

85. J. W. Perry, *The Far Side of Madness* (Englewood Cliffs, NJ: Prentice-Hall, 1974).

86. Ibid., p. 51.

87. Ibid., p. 54.

88. Ibid., p. 9.

89. Ibid., p. 54.

92. G. Rosenthal, "Inflated by the Spirit," in D. Anthony, B. Eckert, & K. Wilber (Eds.), *Spiritual Choices* (New York: Paragon House, 1987).

91. Ibid., p. 318.

92. S. Johnson, *Humanizing the Narcissistic Style* (New York: Norton, 1987).

93. D. Polkinghorne, *Narrative Knowing and the Human Sciences* (Albany, NY: State University of New York Press, 1988), pp. 126, 145, 150, 152.

94. D. MacAdams, *Power, Intimacy, and the Life Story: Personological Inquiries into Identity* (Homewood, IL: Dorsey Press, 1985), pp. 2, 8.

95. Ibid., pp. 18–9, 25.

96. Ibid., p. 134.

97. Ibid., p. 142.

98. A. Maslow, *Toward a Psychology of Being* (2nd ed.) (New York: Van Nostrand, 1968), p. 136.

99. D. MacAdams, op cit., p. 164.

100. Ibid., p. 142.

101. For more on apprenticeship and mentorship see D. Levinson, *The Seasons of a Man's Life* (New York: Ballantine, 1978), and G. Bogart, "Separating From a Spiritual Teacher," *Journal of Transpersonal Psychology, 24* (1992): 1–21.

102. L. Cochran, *The Sense of Vocation: A Study of Career and Life Development* (Albany: State Universtiy of New York Press, 1990), p. 40.

103. Ibid., p. 92.

104. Ibid., p. 95.

105. R. Dass, & P. Gorman, *How Can I Help?* (New York: Knopf, 1985).

106. S. Grof, *The Holotropic Mind* (San Francisco: Harper Collins, 1993).

107. B. Wittine, "Beyond Ego," *Yoga Journal, 76* (1987): 52–3.

108. S. Grof, op cit.

109. H. Kohut, op cit.

110. K. Wilber, "Two Patterns of Transcendence: A Reply to Washburn," *Journal of Humanistic Psychology, 30 (1990): 113–36.*

111. J. Wellwood, "Reflections on Psychotherapy, Focusing, and Meditation," *Journal of Transpersonal Psychology, 12* (1980): 127–41. Also see J. Engler, "Therapeutic Aims in Psychotherapy and Meditation," in K. Wilber, J. Engler, & D. P. Brown (Eds.), *Transformations of Consciousness (Boston: Shambala, 1986).*

112. S. Aurobindo, *The Synthesis of Yoga* (Pondicherry, India: Sri Aurobindo Ashram, 1972).

About the Author

Greg Bogart is a licensed Marriage, Family, and Child Counselor and maintains a private psychotherapy practice in Berkeley, California. He graduated from Wesleyan University with a degree in Religious Studies. He received his Master's degree in Counseling Psychology from the California Institute of Integral Studies, and his doctorate in Psychology from Saybrook Institute. Greg is an adjunct faculty member at Rosebridge Graduate Institute of Integrative Psychology. He has been a practitioner of yoga since 1972 and teaches at the Yoga School of San Francisco. He also leads weekly dream groups and teaches meditation. He has been a speaker at national conventions of the American Psychological Association and the Association for Humanistic Psychology. His writings have appeared in *The American Journal of Psychotherapy*, *The Journal of Humanistic Psychology*, *The Journal of Transpersonal Psychology*, *The California Therapist*, *The Journal of the Society for the Study of Dreams*, and *Yoga Journal*.

In addition to his work as a counselor, writer, and educator, Greg is a musician and song-writer. He currently resides in the hills of Wildcat Canyon, Richmond, California.

Greg Bogart is available for lectures, workshops, and personal consultations. If you would like to contact him, please write to him c/o Dawn Mountain Press, P.O. Box 9563, Berkeley, CA 94709.

Index of Names